Sisters of the World

The Story of Soromundi Lesbian Chorus of Eugene

Ann Roberts

Kate Barry

The events and conversations in this book have been set down to the best of the authors' ability, although some names and details have been changed to protect the privacy of individuals.

For rights and permissions, please contact:

Soromundi Lesbian Chorus of Eugene

PO Box 40934

Eugene, Oregon 97404

info@soromundi.org

ISBN (ebook): 979-8-9988751-0-6

ISBN (paperback): 979-8-9988751-1-3

To Karm Hagedorn, whose vision and determination created an incredible organization that left an indelible mark on the LGBTQ+ community and the city of Eugene.

To Dr. Lisa Hellemn, whose unequaled talent, patience, and teaching ability gave—and continues to give—life to Karm's vision, every Tuesday night.

And to all the Mundis, past and present, thank you for raising your voices in song, risking your reputations and lives during troubled times, and telling our stories through the universal language of music.

Acknowledgments

A memoir is a series of personal recollections, and many people shared their lives and stories, starting with Karm and Lisa. They allowed us to interview them multiple times, and they relived some difficult moments. The presidents of the modern-era Board of Directors, Linda Cipriano, Amber Smith, Kate Barry, and Micki Varner, came together for a lively exchange of the last eighteen years. Thank you to all the current and past Mundis and community members who shared their stories through interviews and other communications.

Karin Hansen and Mary Robertson poured over thousands of photos, several pages of which are included on our YouTube channel at: https://tinyurl.com/soromundibook

We give a shoutout to all the past and present chorus members who let us borrow their memorabilia so we could cobble together a timeline of events and have tangible artifacts to reference at certain points of the narrative.

Dr. Judith Raiskin and Dr. Linda Long created the *Outliers and Outlaws* project at the University of Oregon, which inspired this project. They coined the term, "Lesbian Mecca" as it applies to Eugene.

We are grateful to the Oregon Community Foundation whose grant supported Soromundi's commemorations of their 35th year.

Author KC Luck guided us through the self-publication process, ensuring our little non-profit could create an affordable final product.

Thank you to our spouses for putting up with us during the last eighteen months!

Authors' Notes

Ann Roberts

When my wife and I moved to Eugene, Oregon, in the spring of 2017, we knew no one except our Realtor and Soromundi member, Rebecca Swing. The chorus was a month away from its spring concert, and during casual follow-up with Rebecca, she learned I liked to sing and suggested we attend the concert, "Broadway." We got our tickets and were excited to do something that didn't involve unpacking or remodeling the fixer-upper house we now called home. We thought it would be fun. We went and...

I was ready to join the chorus by intermission.

The last seven years with Soromundi has reinvigorated my love of music, led me to friendships that will last a lifetime, and settled my wife and I into a community of our people. Writing this memoir doesn't seem to balance the scales, given everything I've received from Soromundi, but it's a start.

I'm so grateful to Kate Barry who has taught me much about the chorus and a time in Lesbian history I only had read about. We are a balance to each other, and in the process, I've gained a great friend and mentor.

Most of my readers know that I write with the encouragement of my wife, Amy, and this one is especially meaningful because she loves the chorus as much as I do. For the last 18 months, she gave up her garage, the dining room table (most flat surfaces, actually), and lots of wall space. She's a keeper.

Kate Barry

I came to Eugene from England in the seventies, initially for grad school, but I stayed and made a life here. I joined Soromundi in 1994; it was only a year since Karm had left and Lisa's second year of directing. As you'll read here, these early years had struggles, but I really wanted to sing especially with a women's chorus. Thirty-one years later I would find it hard to imagine life without Soromundi. Through the years I've been a section leader, tour committee chair, concerts chair, and board president for six years, as well as singing as an alto and now a tenor.

I'm happily married to Barb, who also joined the chorus. My daughter is in Soromundi which is a special joy, and I am lucky enough to have three grandchildren close by. We also have a seventy-eight-pound labradoodle named Jax who has a special place in this memoir since he lay under our living room table for the majority of the interviews that are the foundation of this book.

I have also really appreciated working with Ann, my co-conspirator in this Soromundi 35th History Project. Here's to many years of continued friendship.

FOREWORD

What follows is an attempt to accurately convey the experiences of one very determined, strong, hardy, and empathetic organization that has endured for thirty-six years. That's two generations working on a third. As the saying goes, "We remember moments, not days." We've done our best to chronicle the moments, share the feelings, and tell the story. The folks we've quoted have signed off on the quotations, and they stand by what they say. But you can only interview so many people, and even the moments the interviewees remembered were sometimes gilded by time. Of course, many of those who shared their musical talent have left us. Hopefully we honor their memory by accurately painting the picture of the chorus they loved.

We have *a collection of photos* that accompany this story, but to keep the cost of the book reasonable, we opted to place them on Soromundi's YouTube channel at: https://tinyurl.com/soromundibook

Subscribe to the channel as we promise to continuously add more photos, performances, and interesting history and facts in the coming months!

In addition to hearing and seeing Soromundi on YouTube, you can learn more about Soromundi at https://soromundi.org.

ONE

Buses, vans, cars, and motorcycles cruised northbound from Eugene in a pilgrimage to the 1988 Portland Gay Pride. From the cassette player, Cris Williamson and Meg Christian provided sing-along inspiration, while Freddie Mercury rocked the route in the passing lane. Some pilgrims were bold enough to affix rainbow flags or pink triangles to their bumpers, and for others, reaching the Portland destination would begin the celebration.

Thirty-four-year-old Pat Shirley traveled the route that day. She had joined up with some friends and made the two-hour drive to Oregon's largest and most liberal city. Although Eugene was a well-known destination for lesbians by the late '80s, it didn't have a Pride celebration of its own until 1991.

"I didn't always go," Pat explains, "but for some reason that year, I wanted to be a part of Pride." As the forecast predicted a sunny day, it most likely contributed to her decision.

Pat had arrived in Eugene in 1978 when her partner at the time chose the University of Oregon (U of O) for her graduate program. Pat, who had just graduated from South Carolina with a degree in sociology, was fine with the move. "There were two lesbian destinations--Northampton, Massachusetts, and Eugene, Oregon. My partner's friend lived in Eugene and said there were plenty of bike paths and lesbians. It did not disappoint."

On that sunny June day, the ride to Portland proved to be a great warmup act for the main attraction: the Portland Pride Parade. Once they arrived at the parade route, Pat wandered through the crowd, parting from her friends and soaking up the out-and-proud vibe on the one day the gay and lesbian community claimed as their own.

In a truly serendipitous moment, she found herself on the crowded sidewalk with Karm Hagedorn and Sheryl Bernheine, Karm's wife. Although Pat and Karm were not close friends, they knew each other from numerous social activities and local music events.

The parade headed toward them, and everyone on their corner craned their necks to watch the approach. Grand Marshall Paulette Goodman, a Jewish woman who had grown up in Nazi-occupied Paris and who became the national Parents and Friends of Lesbians and Gays (PFLAG) president, waved to the cheering crowds. Eventually, the Portland Lesbian Chorus (PLC) slowly passed by. Pat remembers, "They were singing a ballad and had given it a double meaning. It was something about not loving a man or never loving a man how I love you."

In fact, the song was "The Way That I Want to Touch You" made famous by Captain and Tennille in 1975. Since only a few artists routinely sang about the queer experience, PLC's flipped version of this hetero song delighted the crowd.

Caught up in the moment, Pat remarked to Karm, "Wouldn't it be great to have this in Eugene?" or, as Karm remembers it, "You should start a choir in Eugene!"

Karm nodded and said, "I was just thinking that myself. Maybe when I get out of school...I'll call you."

Pat didn't give the exchange another thought, but Karm continued to mull it over. "It stayed on the front burner, and I wasn't hesitant," Karm explains. "I just wasn't sure how to go about it, but I knew I wanted a chorus where the music was arranged for the full range of female voices."

Karm had returned to the U of O as a "lifelong learner," working toward a degree in sociology, women's studies, and English. She had a year left and was juggling multiple responsibilities, including work, school, and singing in the U of O Gospel Choir. She had been singing since she was a child and learned harmony from her parents. "I was an only [child], and we'd go on weekend trips, and we'd sing three-part harmony. My mom was always the melody, and my dad would take harmony, and when I'd join in he'd say, 'Nope. You're on my note.' And then I'd find mine. That's how I learned."

She joined the high school chorus, participated in community theater, and in college she performed with a gospel chorus and a women's chorus. "My voice was always low. Even in high school I sang lower than the second altos, so I sang tenor with the boys. Eventually, when I started arranging music, I also added a bass part for women who sang in that range. Lots of women appreciated it." She closely watched the conductors of her choruses and felt confident she could do the same—if she had the opportunity.

The following August Karm earned her degree—and called Pat.

———

On Thursday, September 21, 1989, the first rehearsal of what would become Soromundi Lesbian Chorus of Eugene was held in Karm and Sheryl's living room, in a big pink house on

Seventeenth and Lincoln, near downtown Eugene. Karm and Sheryl had mentioned the idea to Brooke and Millie, two of Sheryl's workmates who liked to sing, and Pat brought her friend Adelka, for a total of six inaugural members.

Karm pulled out her copy of The Beatles' White Album and played "Blackbird." They sang the melody and tried some harmony. They also discussed other songs they liked. They all knew "You'll Never Walk Alone" so they gave that a try as well.

As that first rehearsal ended, everyone agreed to meet again, but no one thought to take a picture to commemorate the first practice. "At the time, we had no idea what we had started or that it would last so long," recalls Pat. "If we'd known [the staying power of the group], maybe I should've asked Karm, 'Wouldn't it be great to have world peace?'"

The group grew by word-of-mouth and bounced around from living room to living room, but by late October, they needed a larger place—one that had risers so all the members could see Karm. In January they moved into the general music room at Whiteaker School. Despite the mounting political turmoil against gays and lesbians, there wasn't any concern from the school district about renting a space to lesbians. By now the group had grown to seventeen. There were no auditions, so the women who joined had varying musical experience and exposure. As has always been the case for Soromundi, some women were focused on musical excellence while others were drawn to the group because of the community of women. Some had just come out. Pamela McGilvray remembers, "I hadn't even kissed a girl yet. It was a little awkward [for me] at first, but I got through it. I just wanted to sing. That was fun."

They had no accompanist, so all songs were sung acapella. They had no sheet music, so they used the oral traditional style with Karm teaching by ear. Karm would sing a line, and the women would sing it back until a song was learned in three-part harmony. "We picked songs we liked, songs that weren't difficult for me to arrange," Karm states. She provided lyric sheets, and on her copy, she included symbols, indicating whether the music went up or down so she could remember what she taught.

They divided into high, medium, and low voices. As Karm said, "God forbid you call a lesbian a soprano." Most rehearsals brought a lot of questions and chit chat, given the newness of the group and the different motives for attendance.

According to one Mundi, "The songs were simpler, but there were a lot of interruptions. It was annoying. I thought people should be paying attention."

As more and more women found the fledgling chorus, the yearning to perform increased. Karm, though, was less enthusiastic. "My joy was in the rehearsing. I wasn't ever hot to perform, but I was grateful people wanted to hear us."

Sharing their music with an audience brought up a multitude of questions. What is our name? What do we wear? How do we publicize ourselves? Soon after the initial rehearsal, business meetings began to discuss these organizational topics. After standing for ninety minutes, those desiring to participate in the meeting after rehearsal would sit down on the Whiteaker school risers. Leadership was organic and anything that was viewed as patriarchal structure was not allowed. Topics varied, there was no written agenda, and concerns and questions about the music itself were fair game as well. Everyone had an equal voice, and in order to hear everyone's opinion, sometimes the business meetings were longer than the chorus practice.

Regarding a name, many ideas were suggested, such as FYRE Choir, but initially the group decided to be the Eugene Lesbian Liberty Chorus. There was never a question that the word lesbian would be in the name. Karm comments, "I always intended it [the chorus] to be political. We lived in times where we needed to make a statement."

In January of 1990, the chorus gave its first performance at the Unitarian Universalist Church, which invited guest performers each month. They performed three songs, and as expected, were well received by the congregation. Their second performance was at International Women's Day on March 8th. Standing on the mall in the pouring rain, the chorus recognized the stakes were higher. Karm states, "Anytime we sing for the Unitarians, [who tend to be accepting of diversity], it's preaching to the choir; however, when you're downtown, you don't know who's out there [in the audience]. A principal seeing a teacher singing under a banner of a lesbian chorus might think, 'Hmm.'"

Eventually the chorus reexamined the name, and while "lesbian" would remain, they found another, more powerful choice. Cheris Kramarae, a guest professor in sociology at the U of O, had published *The Feminist Dictionary* where Karm found the term "soromundi," the name of a far-off star, and whose Latin-rooted meaning is "sisters of the world." The search was over and Soromundi Lesbian Chorus of Eugene (SLCE) was born. Members were and are still known as Mundis (pronounced Moondies).

"The name forced some members to step aside from performing," Anne Donahue remembers. "Five or ten would rehearse but not perform. They were afraid for their jobs or their housing." At the time "moral turpitude" clauses were common in contracts of public employees in education, health care, and government, forcing those who worked in the public sector either to step back in the closet when it came time to sing in public—or to come out.

During practice Karm rehearsed the entire group and then asked those who weren't performing to step aside during the final preparations. Max chose to use this as motivation to come out. "I knew I wanted to sing in the chorus the following September, so I chose to come out," she says. "Some people said, 'Oh, I knew!'"

Over the years the name has continued to invite mixed reactions. Often the reaction was positive and supportive, but the opposite also occurred. Some announcers were uncomfortable saying the entire name, specifically the word *lesbian.* So, sometimes the chorus was introduced simply as Soromundi or Soromundi Women's Chorus.

Karm had no problem correcting anyone who mispronounced Soromundi or who failed to say the entire name—including the word lesbian. Pat laughs, "I lost track of how many times Karm would grab the microphone from somebody and remind them we were the *lesbian* chorus of Eugene."

In one case, after having sung at several Martin Luther King (MLK) celebrations, the chorus was suddenly uninvited. At another performance, the manager of a hall where the chorus was due to perform called to ask if the word "lesbian" could be dropped from the concert name and publicity. More frequently, the choir would simply find their name had been changed in the program or written announcements.

Times have slowly changed. Soromundi was invited to sing the "National Anthem" during a 2017 Veteran's Day ceremony in Springfield, Eugene's more conservative sister city. They were there for the unveiling of the statue honoring Oregon women in the military. Former Mundis, who were veterans, were out in force to see the statue, "Lioness," and hear the chorus sing. Further invitations to sing "The National Anthem" came from the U of O Women's Basketball organization and the local minor league baseball team's Pride event.

However, there have been setbacks as recently as 2019 when Soromundi was slated to sing with a local gospel choir for a church service where that choir rehearsed. A few days before the concert, when the president of the board heard the chorus's name and realized lesbians would be singing at the church, he disinvited them. Soromundi reached out to a pastor at a different church who was happy to host both choruses, since the other chorus refused to perform without Soromundi. As a result, the gospel choir also decided to change their rehearsal venue to a more inclusive, welcoming church.

When Soromundi appeared, often the name forced audiences to acknowledge their homophobia and confront it. After hearing a few songs, though, many audience members visibly softened their body language, and the judgment and disdain melted. Many Mundis recalled a lunchtime performance for a local business group as an important and visible change in audience perspective. Rebecca Swing remembers, "Once we were invited to sing for one of the Eugene Rotary chapters. I knew people in the audience, most of them fifty to eighty years old. Some Mundis couldn't come [because they weren't out] and so we only had twenty-five to thirty singers. We got a great reception, and by the end there were people crying." (As was learned later, several Rotary members didn't attend because of the lesbian chorus.)

Regarding the same performance for the Rotary, Harriet Merrick adds, "After so many years of giving speeches, I can read a room. I remember walking in and thinking, Oh, shit. This will be a hard sell. What I saw was the shift. One person came up to me afterward and said, 'I just need you to know how important that was.'"

Diana Bailey had a difficult decision, when Soromundi traveled to sing in her town, Roseburg. The "Roseburg Mundis" were featured with a full-page photo on the cover of the entertainment section of the local paper that weekend, and Diana was due to start a new job the following week. She decided to sing with the group at a local church, and she wouldn't let fear rule her, and she didn't hide. "On Monday," she explains, "I took a deep breath and walked into my new job. I was greeted by the chaplain and asked how the concert went. Others were friendly and a few were quiet. Those few were the ones I worked with over several years, and I bonded with them as we discovered our commonalities."

———

The group's third performance was at the Eugene Celebration. The Celebration was launched in 1983 by Cynthia "Cindy" Wooten, city councilor, state legislator, and general Eugene mover and shaker, to celebrate the opening of the Hult Center, a 22.5-million-dollar performance venue. The Hult put Eugene on the map as a serious player in the performing arts. The Celebration was a massive community street party in early September with a legendary parade and multiple open air music venues. Streets were closed off with food trucks, public service booths, and other vendors. It was such a hit that it became a yearly event until 2014 when it was no longer feasible to produce.

Sitting in the audience for Soromundi's performance was Lisa Hellemn, a lifelong musician, who, after completing her master's in music, would later obtain her doctorate in education at the U of O. At the time, she was taking a break from teaching music, and she'd started classwork at U of O, but she still lived in Yachats. She remembers, "I just heard about the Celebration, so I wanted to take it in and check out the lesbian culture. I was directed to the L&L Market to watch the parade, and then I wandered downtown. When I saw the group, and I've seen a million choirs, I wasn't that interested at first, but I noticed as people wandered by, they slowed to take in a big group of lesbians. It seemed that initially they viewed it as a spectacle, but then their stereotypes were immediately broken down. I think they left the scene with different opinions. That's powerful."

Lisa was intrigued by the chorus's two-part and three-part harmony. "They were having so much fun and singing songs I knew...It was a different experience for me. That was awesome. They were part activist, part social, and part entertainment. I could envision them changing minds in one fell swoop. They could have an unsuspecting audience and completely change their minds about *what* lesbians are and *who* is lesbian."

Afterward, Lisa found Karm surrounded by the chorus members and an enthusiastic audience. Some were basking in the post-performance high and others had questions. She managed to get Karm's attention long enough to ask if they needed an accompanist. While Karm doesn't really remember the words exchanged, Lisa says, "She was so busy and only gave me a brief reply, but she did, though, give me their rehearsal information. So I just took the initiative and showed up to the next rehearsal. I thought I could be a great asset, and they just didn't know it yet," she remembers with a laugh.

When Lisa arrived at rehearsal, she was handed a lyric sheet and nothing else, since the chorus was still married to the oral tradition model. "I wasn't used to playing without music, but fortunately it was straightforward, and I could figure out some chords." Lisa also listened to Karm's arrangement and transcribed what was being sung. After a few rehearsals they were a team.

"It was lifechanging," Karm states. "We could start singing something and she'd just start playing like she does."

Lisa seemed to be the missing piece, providing warmups, supporting sections, and writing transcriptions to support Karm's work. This ensured that the same vocal parts could be replicated the next week.

However, not everyone was immediately thrilled with

Lisa's arrival. "I wasn't part of the lesbian feminist movement," Lisa remembers. "I lived over on the coast in Yachats. This was a different atmosphere. I saw that the more they [the chorus] got together, the stronger they were, and as they became stronger, they felt empowered. They started challenging Karm. It was only my second rehearsal when someone said, 'I don't like the sound of the piano,' and people started questioning the need for an accompanist."

Karm ignored any questions and concerns. She knew Lisa's value, and many Mundis did as well. Pat adds, "She brought so much. How many acapella songs can one group sing?"

Once she moved to Eugene, Lisa also experienced the impact that the group's name had on more conservative people. "I was in the gospel choir at U of O for a couple of years, and a friend invited me to her church. There was a guest pastor who decided to make his sermon about how sinful this community was because there was a choir called Soromundi Lesbian Chorus of Eugene, and they were out to recruit people. It was strange to sit in the congregation as we were named as the scourges of the area by this visiting pastor. Of course, my friend was horrified."

The experience foreshadowed the very unpredictable and mixed reactions Soromundi would receive from religious communities throughout their thirty-five-plus years of existence—angry protesters or empty pews but also standing ovations and changed minds.

Two

Most of the women who joined Soromundi in those first few years had arrived in Eugene between the late '60s and mid-'80s when thousands of lesbians migrated to Oregon, specifically to Eugene, which became a Lesbian Mecca.[1] Young women swept up in the growing national counterculture not only yearned to abandon the ways of their parents, but they also wanted to find people like themselves.

San Francisco and New York City had become the epicenters of the burgeoning gay rights and feminist movements, including radical lesbian feminism, which encouraged separatism and a complete denunciation of the patriarchy. As women moved to Oregon, they brought many of these ideas with them. As part of their new-found freedom, women often adopted names such as Seagull or Gypsy. While many enjoyed the trappings of a city community, others went off the grid on what became known as womyn's land. In the '70s, Oregon's land was reasonably priced, especially when compared with its neighbor, California. Women who had inherited money were the purchasers and the land went into a trust that served the experimental collectives. Rootworks, Cabbage Lane, Rainbow's End, Owl Farm, and Women's Share were the closest womyn's land communities to Eugene, each one with a unique story but with striking similarities—a commitment to consensus, feminism, freedom, and women-only space.

Mundi Kay Christopher recalls, "I wound up there by accident. In 1976 my partner at the time had gone up I-5 in our VW van and broken down on the side of the road. Stacy, a woman living at Rootworks and working at Keto's Garage in Wolf Creek, picked her up and helped her get back on the road. I came up there to check it out and ended up living there in a little cabin." She smiles and adds, "It was a lot of fun. One summer Cabbage Lane declared it was Single Summer and no woman was allowed to be in an exclusive relationship. If you wanted to sleep with someone, you had to pick a name out of a hat. I'd met someone living at Cabbage Lane, and she would sneak over to my place during Single Summer."

Consensus was the accepted way of decision-making and problem-solving. This protocol requires that no decision is made that a member cannot accept. Since every person's opinion is valued and considered, consensus-building often demands lengthy conversation and debate on a single issue. This was also the culture of Soromundi's early years.

Kay eventually moved to Eugene to attend mechanics' school, leaving behind her rustic way of life for a large house and five roommates. Although the living arrangements were quite a shift, she found the Eugene women's community shared the same values she'd found on womyn's land. The influx of lesbians to Eugene led to the creation of women-owned businesses that were often solely staffed by women, and like their counterparts on womyn's land, they ran the businesses based on the tenets of radical feminism. They created a microcosm within the larger, university-centered town. At the time it seemed like a feminist utopia; a lesbian could essentially avoid males and the patriarchy all day since women-owned restaurants, bookstores, and even a construction company flourished. Feminist cooperatives operated with alternative economics. People bartered, and in some cases, each worker took from the profits just what she needed in that moment; some took more, some took less.

Harriet states, "We had to build our own culture, our own community. No one was looking out for us. We were on our own. That happened in businesses, in attitudes, and later you saw it in Soromundi too."

In Oregon the U.S. Forest Service provided a golden opportunity for hippies and others in the back-to-the-land movement. Hoedads, a worker-owned cooperative tree planting company, co-founded by Jerry Rust, used the need for reforestation to plant trees throughout the Willamette Valley. The Hoedads were committed to a collaborative work model, environmentalism, and feminism. Among the two dozen-plus laboring Hoedad crews, an all-lesbian crew called Full Moon Rising was formed. "We worked by the tree or by the share [an hourly amount]," Mundi Myeba Mindlin explains. "The tree planters were respected, and there was a lot of singing on the crew, a lot of circle singing."

Circle songs are created through improvisation and collaboration. A leader calls out an uplifting verse that a few people repeat before the leader moves to the next line, usually adding a harmony. Eventually all join and the song comes full circle. Engaging in such an activity made the days pass much faster for this extremely strenuous and difficult work. It connected the planters to each other in such a way that only music could.

Kay explains, "I had heard that on hot days women went shirtless and there was a *lot* going on in the forest. Then at the end of the day they headed to the laundromat, completely covered in dirt and mud."

Different lesbian groups and organizations offered options

for after-work gathering. Amazon Kung Fu taught self-defense and The Wallflower Order created political dance pieces that defied the norms of what a dancer could look like and what they could perform. Mundi Sally Sheklow wrote a musical titled, *The Sound of Lesbians*, a parody of *The Sound of Music*. Lisa traveled around with Sally performing it throughout Oregon communities and at women's festivals. It was so popular that word eventually reached Rodgers and Hammerstein, the composers of the Julie Andrews' classic, and their attorneys instructed Sheklow to cease and desist—or face legal action. Later, WYMPROV, a lesbian comedy improv group that Sally co-founded, was incredibly popular with multiple audiences and performed for over two decades.

The Women's Press and the *Lavender Network* chronicled the life of the women's community, and Ovulars, a photography studio, validated "real" women and included well-known artist Tee Corinne. At the epicenter of the women's community was the feminist bookstore, Mother Kali's. Throughout its thirty-three-year existence at three different locations, Mother Kali's (named after a Hindi goddess) served as the unofficial "Lesbian Mecca Chamber of Commerce." Women new to the area were quickly steered to Mother Kali's —and Izzy Harbaugh, the longtime manager of the store, who often donated her salary to help keep the store in the black. The original space was a former house, so it already looked like home, and each woman entering Mother Kali's needed something—a book, a conversation, advice, or information. Izzy recognized each woman's needs and steered them in the right direction. She had the ability to empathize and understand each person.

Most information at "Mother K's" was shared on the bulletin board. A sea of multi-colored flyers with pull-off tabs announced houses and rooms to rent, available jobs and services for hire, bartering and trading for goods, and all the special events happening soon, such as a Soromundi concert. As the manager, Izzy oversaw all of it with her partner and Mundi Lorraine Ironplow, and her name became synonymous with the bookstore. When she passed in 1999, Soromundi sang at her memorial, which had to be relocated to the Lane Events Center to accommodate the crowd. The bookstore attempted to carry on in some different iterations but eventually closed.

Mother Kali's, though, lasted longer than the other businesses. Many were the victims of capitalism and simple economics. For example, once mainstream grocery stores began to carry organic foods, at a lower price than goods distributed by lesbian collective Starflower, the customers followed the savings, and Starflower closed its doors.

As the Lesbian Mecca period ended, Soromundi was just beginning, its membership drawing from every corner of the community, including some lesbians from womyn's land. Many members saw Soromundi as a space for fostering empowerment, growing their voices, and healing from a marginalized status. They embraced many of the same tenets, including circle songs. The songs sung in the mountains and chanted at pagan festivals became a cornerstone of Soromundi's early repertoire.

With the demise of lesbian organizations, some Mundis realized that changes were necessary to ensure the organization survived. While linchpin issues might be best served through consensus, using this model to solve small, everyday disagreements wasn't practical. Soromundi also had an additional challenge. While some decisions were made as an organization, more decisions were musical decisions, which were traditionally made by the musical director. Some Mundis recognized the need for multiple decision-making and problem-solving strategies, but many steadfastly held to their understanding of consensus as the only way.

Adding to the stress within the group was the malignant homophobia raging throughout Oregon, as fundamental right-wingers attacked gays and lesbians at every ballot box available. A slew of ballot measures was generated during the late '80s and early '90s by a group called Oregon Citizens Alliance (OCA). Its leaders peppered communities, cities, and the state with more than thirty-five referendums, all of which were designed to strip the gay and lesbian community of civil rights. Many of the local measures passed by enormous margins, only fueling OCA's cause. Soromundi's commitment to being out and proud would face many challenges in the coming year, as one of the most important laws to the Oregon queer community would come up for review.

In 1972, during the Lesbian Mecca period, the Oregon Legislature decriminalized homosexuality, but the gay and lesbian community knew there was—and always had been—prejudice that no piece of legislation could quickly extinguish. Harriet explains, "In those days the cops were not our friends. We knew not to walk alone after dark when we were leaving The Riv [the Riviera Room, a gay and lesbian bar] because the game 'Roll a Queer' was common."

A native Oregonian, Harriet has spent her entire adult life advocating, campaigning, volunteering, advising, and teaching about gay rights. She arrived in Eugene in the early '70s, a student at the U of O, with an internship that allowed her to study community public service, an opportunity few universities offered.

She has served on dozens of boards, helmed several organizations, and was the named plaintiff in *Merrick v. Oregon*, a 1992 case that reached the Oregon Court of Appeals. The Court ruled in her favor and overturned Measure 8, an OCA ballot measure of the late '80s that stripped protection from anyone in the gay and lesbian community who worked at the "executive level," such as the U of O, where Harriet was employed.

The OCA systematically moved from conservative rural communities to larger areas, fueling the development of Measure 9. It was perhaps the boldest and most dangerous. It would have amended the state constitution to equate homosexuality to pedophilia. Schools would be required to "set standards for Oregon youth that recognized homosexuality as abnormal, wrong, unnatural, and perverse."

As Eugene had passed non-discrimination legislation in the '70s, which was later repealed by Measure 51, Measure 9 proved to be a hotbed of struggle since both sides felt they could win. The gay and lesbian community turned out in force—knocking on doors, staging rallies, and talking to their neighbors. Of course, protesting Measure 9 meant being visible and often the queer community was subjected to verbal and physical violence. As chronicled in the award-winning 1995 film, *Ballot Measure 9*, businesses owned by gays and lesbians were trashed and neighbors were far less than neighborly, vandalizing property, and in one heinous example, blinding a pet horse with a pitchfork.[2]

Harriet remembers, "A lot of dangerous things happened on those campaigns. Some of the volunteers couldn't do another campaign, so we were constantly looking for new people because so many had been verbally and physically threatened."

As Soromundi was in the process of applying for 501(c)3 status, the chorus couldn't take a specific political stance, but they could be visible and support their community by battling the stereotypes. They sang at International Women's Day, the Willamette Valley Folk Festival, as well as rallies and protests at Springfield City Hall, the Eugene Federal Building, MLK Celebrations, Take Back the Night, and Eugene Pride. They tried to sing anywhere they were invited, such as churches and civic meetings, prioritizing access to the general population. Their visibility combated the OCA propaganda sent to churches.

Soromundi's active phone tree ensured they could be ready to perform in less than twenty-four hours, and they proudly raised their voices for victims of violence and suffering. They drove out to Junction City to sing at the deathbed of a man dying from AIDS and sang at a vigil for two lesbians who'd been murdered in Medford, Oregon. A frequent mantra adopted was, "Who will sing for the women who cannot? We will!"

The work and sacrifice by the lesbian and gay community, as well as their allies, paid off. Measure 9 failed, fifty-six percent of the state voting against it with most of those "no" votes deriving from the urban areas. Many Mundis participated in a celebration of the defeat.

———

Amidst the social turmoil, Soromundi Lesbian Chorus of Eugene continued to grow. Within a few years the non-audition chorus had grown to nearly forty, and the members' dual motivations of singing and joining a community became quite apparent. While many in the chorus wanted both, some women were there just to make friends—or find a girlfriend. Soromundi became a 501(c)3 and loosely formed a board of directors, although there was no desire to create any structure that resembled a "patriarchal board." They held strong to the principle of consensus regarding where to sing, what to sing, and how to dress, which made for very long business meetings. Pat recalls, "Most of us didn't know how to be a chorus member, and we lacked a real structure. So, everybody's needs came out all over the place. I could see dealing with the membership was stressful [for Karm and Lisa]."

If one ingredient for success is using all your tools and the advantages you have, then Soromundi lucked out with Karm. As the events manager for the Hult Center, Karm had learned what made a professional performer and hoped to steer Soromundi in that direction. For their spring concert in May of 1992, they performed in the Hult Center's Soreng Theater. Karm's charisma and charm had won over the various staff at the Hult, who assured her Soromundi's production would be the best it could be. Karm adds, "I held the calendar, and I was very careful to keep my work time and Soromundi time separate."

The Soreng only seats 495 people, but technically it provides everything found in its much larger counterpart, the Silva. The Soreng is perfect for local performing groups and artists, whose audience draw is usually smaller and whose performance dates are fewer. It has a balcony as well as tiered seating, and its asymmetrical architecture creates an intimacy between performers and audience.

Karm says, "I'll never forget the first time the chorus went into the Soreng for our tech rehearsal. It was May 9, 1992."

"Some people had never been there," Lisa adds, "and since our chorus was open to a wide range of people with a wide range of experiences or sometimes a lack of experiences, many were agog. They were testing out the sound backstage by making all kinds of noises to see what it was like. There were people getting on the stage and then going off [into the audience] to see the stage. People studied the upholstered seats. It was so impactful that people had trouble focusing on Karm."

"I knew it was important," Karm concludes. "Their reaction as they walked into a professional theater...It was worth any amount we paid, and I knew it would yield great things."

While the spring concert in the Soreng was a highlight of the third season, behind the scenes, the group was struggling. It was suggested that the chorus engage in consensus training.

It had become apparent that while everyone claimed to know what that was, many had different understandings, which was a central problem the group confronted every time they discussed an issue. Soromundi organized a retreat around the topic, the takeaway being that consensus required compromise and not everyone in the group needed to agree, but the decision couldn't ask anyone to go beneath her bottom line. While the "thumbs up" activity was adopted after that meeting, Lisa didn't notice much difference, and the tension and mistrust amidst the group continued. "I think people wanted to voice their opinion more than direct the course of things, but they wanted to be heard and have some power."

The problems and mistrust would soon cause a major break in the organization.

THREE

The fourth season, 1992-1993, began with heightened social and political turmoil as the vote on Measure 9 was still two months away. The gay and lesbian community faced immense pressure to retreat to the closet, and they had endured acts of violence and faced workplace discrimination. It was inevitable the stress and anguish would permeate each week's rehearsal, adding to the existing mistrust directed at Karm and amplifying the need to be heard. All the personalities within the group were emerging, as well as the inability to separate personal life, job, and politics.

This was a new phenomenon for Lisa, as she had traveled a different path than many in the chorus. "I didn't really understand the lesbian separatist thing because I had always found ways to collaborate with other groups of people. I had experienced homophobia and discrimination, so I welcomed cultural space for women, but I didn't understand the lack of trust or the need for everyone to challenge everything."

Karm adds, "I've always believed a lot of life happens between Tuesday nights. For many, Soromundi felt like a safe place, where a lot of life got processed by the chorus."

Many in the chorus couldn't leave personal issues behind when they walked into rehearsal, and no one really had the authority to require them to do so. The natural consequence of giving voice to a disenfranchised group suffering from trauma is that they will eventually unload all the baggage they've been carrying. Since the group rejected anything that looked like patriarchal leadership, no one, not even Karm, was openly anointed as leader. Although Karm, and Lisa, as her support, investigated all the songs suggested by the members, spent hours transcribing the music and words for those songs, and arranged the music to fit the singers' vocal range, their power was limited. Karm faced the chorus each week to conduct the rehearsals, but it was hard to predict what would happen or how much would get accomplished.

Pat explains, "We started to crumble from the weight [needs of the group], without a real structure underneath us. During rehearsal, people constantly asked, 'Can we change this? Do you think you could play those notes differently? Couldn't we sing this part lower?'"

Often these types of suggestions hijacked the rehearsal. Rather than learning music, the rehearsals devolved into discussion or arguments. This fact frustrated many members who understood and believed that some amount of leadership was critical to the end goal—learning a repertoire and performing it in front of an audience. Karm adds, "People felt free to contribute and raise issues. A couple times I had to call for a moratorium and focus on the music and ask them to say stuff after. Sometimes that worked and sometimes it didn't."

"We were growing faster than we could keep up," Lisa says. "There were people in the chorus who wanted to lead. There were people who seemed adamant about expressing themselves, but it was very anti-establishment, very anti-hierarchical, very anti-trust of leaders."

At the same time, Soromundi's reputation led to impressive and important invitations, including an ask from the Willamette Valley Folk Festival and a performance at the Harvey Milk dinner. They sang everywhere, on the mall on International Women's Day, at a National Abortion Rights (NARAL) rally, and at a nursing home.

Amidst the strife of the chorus, on March 8, 1993, International Women's Day, Karm was named Woman of the Year by the Eugene Human Rights Commission. Despite the recognition Karm received for her efforts, after three years of long business meetings, walking the tightrope of consensus, and being challenged about most everything by members of the chorus, Karm was frazzled. She and Sheryl had welcomed their daughter into the world three months earlier, and Karm found herself dreading rehearsal nights and whatever friction awaited her.

"There was so much mistrust that a few people had," she explains, "and they had no limits, no shame or grace. They were just trying to get people riled up. It had to change, and a lot of people refused."

The final straw proved to be an invitation Karm made to a singer/songwriter from Seattle. Previously Karm had arranged for other singers to conduct workshops. For example, Ysaye Barnwell from Sweet Honey in the Rock led a singing workshop with Soromundi that included the Bethel Temple Gospel Chorus and Inspirational Sounds. Yet, this new invitation brought more conflict. "I'd met her at the Motherhood Music Camp and I wanted her to come down and work with us, collaborate with us. I just thought it would be fun, but people asked why I'd invited an outsider, and I was accused of having ulterior motives."

Karm abruptly announced her exit at a rehearsal before a concert in the spring of 1993. "I don't think people ever knew how sad it made me. I've had my detractors, and I could name them to this day, but if I see them on the street, I'll be civil.

But I don't think people realized I felt responsible for so many things. When I asked my new friend [the singer/songwriter from Seattle] to work with us, I just wanted us to be as good as we could be. When those detractors accused me of having my own agenda... How could anyone think that?"

She knew then what she needed to do. "Step aside when you no longer want to carry the bullhorn," Karm states.

"When Karm announced she was leaving, I was stunned," Pat admits. "It was like having the rug pulled out, and I thought she must feel so desperate to do that."

Lisa adds, "I had often wondered how she had tolerated it [the disrespect]. Some people were so focused on their needs and opinions, they hadn't even bothered to understand Karm's. I was surprised by the when, where, and how it [the announcement] occurred, but I wasn't shocked that she had to leave. Karm saw herself as a friend and benevolent leader to these women; that's how it had all started. Then, as more people joined, the more they pushed her out front. Then they abandoned her. Ironically, they felt abandoned by her as well." Because of her teaching and music background, Lisa has always viewed the directorship as a teacher role—a leader. Friendship and relationships happened on a different plane.

Karm acknowledges that perhaps having a beautiful life at home might have been the impetus of the choice to leave, but she's clear that she had room in her schedule and her heart for Soromundi, but not with the contentious conditions that existed. "It wasn't the baby that made my decision," she says. "But I asked myself, 'Why do I need all of this heartache when I can just be home with a baby and be full of joy and happiness?' It was so painful to have done what I did and then have people turn on me."

She felt bad that everything got dumped on Lisa, and many of the founding veteran members left with her, especially those who had joined specifically because Karm was leading Soromundi.

As Karm looks back at that time and the pushback from her detractors, she reflects, "My biggest regret is that I didn't say, 'Cut that shit out.' But at the time, it was too painful. And I had this joy at home...But along the way, I recall times when I wish I would've said, 'If you don't like this, move along.' All I ever wanted was to sing. Here were a few people who got riled up and they're coming after you, and you're being eaten. You're a leader who's being eaten."

"It [Karm's departure] was horrible," Lisa says. "Working with Karm was the most rewarding thing I was getting out of it [being in Soromundi]. Everyone was mistrustful of any type of leadership; if we did anything like another group, it was perceived as patriarchal and traditional. I didn't see a way forward, so when I was asked if I'd stay, I said absolutely not. I felt bad because most of the people left in the room were hoping the chorus would survive. They were feeling abandoned. I told them I would help them through the spring concert, which was going to be held at the Campbell Center. After the concert, they could interview some people for the director's position."

However, it was not smooth sailing. At one of the first rehearsals someone interrupted Lisa to question an aspect of what they were doing. Instead of answering the person directly, she told the chorus they needed to decide what they wanted, and if they wanted her to direct, then they had to let her do that.

Pat remembers, "Lisa said, 'Well, maybe you need to decide as a group who you want *or* what you want for a leader and what type you want, and I'm just going to wait until you have this together.' Then she got up and went and sat in the rows with us and she just sat there and waited and waited and waited...I don't know who was the first to speak up. She eventually went back and led us, and we were quiet."

Lisa worked with the chorus that spring on two levels: preparing them for a modified spring concert and developing a job description for Musical Director, "but the chorus's expectations were completely unrealistic" she recalls. They wanted someone with formal music training, but they didn't want that person to make all the musical decisions. They wanted someone with leadership experience, but they wanted to do all the leading. Eventually, an exhaustive search yielded two potential candidates, but both were ruled out. The chorus leaders approached Lisa again. This time she put forth some conditions, which many in the chorus accepted as fair and logical. She insisted that music become the focus of rehearsals, regardless of the members' motivation for joining, and that she would oversee all musical decisions. She encouraged the general membership to continue to have a say in organizational details such as performance venues and group goals.

"I don't want to say it badly...but being from a musical background, it was hard to stand in front of a group that couldn't sing in tune and didn't know the basics of general music. A part of me just couldn't attach myself to that. But this was part of *my* growth. The teacher part of me wanted to hang in there and bring the group along."

Becoming the director proved challenging for several reasons. In addition to navigating the fragile trust that the chorus leaders extended to her, Lisa grappled with her feelings about her role as leader of a non-audition chorus rooted in lesbian feminism. For a long time, she kept a professional distance while slowly building friendships within the group.

Lisa was initially somewhat dismayed at the ethos of the early chorus. "The whole conformity thing... Why did people need to have short hair? Why do people have to come out to their parents? Why do people have to be in someone's face because they feel differently? I did not understand 'We are so diverse, but we have to all be the same in how we think and how we present.' That's not diversity." Later, in a moment of reflection she adds, "I guess I was disappointed or disillusioned. I assumed every lesbian went through a soul-searching process and broke down the social constructs of sexual orientation, blowing up the fairy tales, so I thought they would also be open to different ways of thinking or feeling or being. Then I found out that some lesbians are more rigid than ever, even after being persecuted for being themselves. I didn't understand or condone the way some viewed the world, yet I was a part of the group. I was young, idealistic, and I just hadn't figured it all out yet. I certainly didn't relate to the whole lesbian separatist thing, but I sure got an education, and started to understand what other people had been through."

Lisa now had a chorus with some major musical deficits. "When Karm left, a lot of the strong core singers left. I'm built to think that if you're not staying, you're not meant to be here. Each week a few more left, so first we had to backtrack. We spent a couple of years just trying to get back musically to where we were and building some trust." That meant returning to simplified music, easy harmonies, and circle songs.

Still, Lisa wanted to progress to more complicated music. "I wanted to carry on the work that Karm had started in terms of elevating the music. Then some new folks landed, and they felt more comfortable with the music and pushing ahead. So we started doing some interesting things with arrangements."

Whether it was Lisa's musical knowledge or having managed hundreds of students, or both, the chorus moved forward because of her leadership. As a committed, non-audition chorus with a wide and varied distribution of musical skills, developing Soromundi was a challenge. However, for Lisa, this challenge was also a strength. "I've always felt like adults don't have access to good performance opportunities unless they're formally trained. And I think that's wrong, because I think what music has to offer, what drama and art have to offer, should be accessible to everybody. So, I loved the non-audition part of it, and that just seemed like an awesome challenge."

Many people in the chorus had been told that they couldn't sing, or for a variety of reasons they were terrified of singing. They had received many negative messages about their musical ability or presumed lack of it. For Lisa music was a great salve or remedy—a therapy—requiring skill and discipline and promoting self-expression. As one Mundi put it, "Singing brings access to joy."

Soromundi continues to be a true community choir. Access to music was and *is* a non-negotiable part of the Soromundi experience. As Karm professes, "If we all sing together, we can all sing."

Lisa employed the strategies she had learned as an educator to help people gain that access and build their skills, but there are still challenges. With a non-audition chorus the measure of ability shifts each year. "The music teacher part of me thought this was doable, and it was just going to take time to build the skills, but people join who don't have all the skills or the same level of skills that some have learned from participating in Soromundi. There are always some who come in September and say, "'I've never sang in a choir, and I don't know what I'm doing.'"

Many chorus members have highlighted Lisa's abilities as director, not just the sense of engagement with the music but also because of the way she uses her formal music education to transmit singing techniques to members who have such a variety of musical backgrounds. She can help people understand how to achieve good pitch, how different mouth shapes will produce different notes and styles of singing. Lisa reminds the chorus to have "big ears," and she can recognize if one person is off key within the whole choral group. She talks about pitch to the group, saying, "Tenors you don't have that line yet," but never singles out an individual.

Mundi and former president Linda Cipriano states, "Lisa can have eighty women in a room with varying musical abilities from 'can't carry a tune in a bucket' to highly trained. She can still make us sound good. It's brilliant. I don't know if anyone else could do that."

As the group made slow progress, it was a time when Soromundi would sing anywhere—churches, banquet halls, even a gymnasium for a performance for the Human Rights Campaign. There were performances for Parents and Friends of Lesbians and Gays (PFLAG), The Gay and Lesbian Alliance Against Defamation (GLAAD), and Clergy and Laity Concerned (CALC). They were asked to celebrate the opening of the Anne Frank exhibit in Cottage Grove, the Dalles, and Sheridan. As their confidence grew, they opened themselves to the idea of more collaborations with other groups.

Lisa remembers, "We wanted to reengage with the community, so in addition to new opportunities, we were doing all the other things that Karm had started, Take Back the Night, the MLK March, the MLK celebration at the Hult Center, the PFLAG banquets. We went anywhere to be of service to the community."

Another important event occurred at this time. Two different researchers landed in Eugene, one to enter a graduate program at the U of O and the other completing a project about lesbian organizations. They asked to interview Lisa, and she agreed to share what she could about Soromundi. While the interviews weren't memorable, Lisa recalls the disturbing news she received. "It seems that some other feminist choirs, like the one in Washington DC, were going through very similar patterns as they grew. Some were breaking into factions or disbanding. Locally the same thing had happened to the Peace Choir, and it seemed to be tied to a clash in opinions or ideology. That's when I decided we needed to attend to the choir's health as an organization, as well as the music."

Fortunately, change was happening as new people joined in the mid-nineties. There was more focus on singing and moving the chorus forward as an organization. The first sign of this was a meeting called by Lisa at the end of the 1994/95 season that focused on chorus goals. After a daylong get together, the leadership/steering committee agreed and developed a "mission statement," although as Lisa recalls, "It couldn't be called that, too military. I shared what I thought the power was—to change hearts and minds. We needed visibility, and we needed to put the music first."

Four

"If we want to be visible, let's take the show on the road," Lisa advised.

Lisa wanted to connect with the outlying communities—the rural towns—where being gay and being out were not synonymous. In 1998, although OCA's statewide ballot measures had been defeated, the group was still active, and after the defeat of Measure 9, they targeted small communities. "I wanted to get out there and battle the stereotypes. Soromundi wasn't created to be activists, but the times demanded that we were. The choice of cities was deliberate. Today they would be called red cities. We used our contacts through Clergy and Laity Concerned (CALC) and PFLAG, and they helped us make arrangements."

A tour committee was formed, but in the spirit of the Soromundi Way, anyone could join in and help. Linda Cipriano, who acted as the tour planner, offers, "We were all leaders and members of the operations or business committee. Everything happened organically."

The committee organized the destinations, the transportation, lodging, and all the performance logistics. It was a five-day tour through Bend, Klamath Falls, Ashland, and Rose-burg. These communities were large enough for the chorus to have support, contacts, and connections, and small enough to have been targeted by the OCA. Everyone would ride together on one bus. Myeba remembers, "I was talking to a woman in the bus office, and I asked if there would be a problem because we were a lesbian singing group. She tells me to hang on and shouts across the room, 'Hey, Mac! It's a bunch of lesbians! Is that okay?'"

Apparently, it was okay. Mac became an invaluable member of the tour, advising about travel times, weather conditions, and giving tips on stowing luggage, risers and musical equipment. He came to every concert, and by the end of the trip, he was named an honorary lesbian.

That April, twenty-two Mundis hopped on the charter bus and headed for their first destination, Bend. One Mundi wasn't out to her family, and another commented that her family didn't even know she was touring with a lesbian chorus. A few Mundis would join them on the way at different locations but having everyone ride on the same bus, created unique opportunities to bond and have fun together. There was much singing in the aisles in small groups and with the whole group, as they practiced for the upcoming performances. Vicki, one of the first straight women to join the chorus, wove baskets and taught anyone willing to learn. Pamela still has a basket from that trip twenty-seven years ago. Wyrda had an "everything back-pack," claiming she had an answer for every possible need. Lisa remembers Max as the "one-liner queen" of the bus, ever ready with her dry humor whenever there was a dull moment.

One constant snag during the tour was getting an accurate headcount for the bus. Linda says, "We hadn't put together a system and we kept getting a different number. When we'd count off, I was always afraid we were leaving someone behind. We rectified this problem by the next tour."

As they journeyed out Highway 126, toward Bend, they made a pitstop at the Belknap Hot Springs, taking over the pool for the afternoon. Bend was the largest city they would visit, the population nearing thirty-five thousand in 1998. They stayed at the Riverside Hotel on the Deschutes River. Rooms were shared, people doubling up to lessen expense. The chorus did not have strong contacts in Bend, and the groups that were supportive were busy planning a civil rights march for that weekend. The chorus arrived at the end of the march and simply joined the ensuing gathering at the downtown park, some still in their suits from Belknap. Later some people relaxed in the hotel or organized games, while another small group headed to the High Desert Museum.

The performance in Bend was at the Sons of Norway Hall, which was not very big and had a low ceiling. However, it did have a working piano and the owners were willing to have the chorus sing there. Lisa explains, "No church would sponsor us." Concert costumes were dark pants or skirts, white shirts, and a vest of your choice. Although there was a good audience, the stop in Bend was not as memorable as the other venues. There was not a feeling of a connected community. Pat recalls, "Perhaps the community was less centralized than I was used to, which then felt to me as less connected. Maybe they were emotionally drained from the day spent protesting, but they seemed less swayed (by the music) and less engaged with us."

Lisa recalls, "The only song they really responded to was 'Full Moon of Love,' but that's probably because they knew the tune and could sing along."

Before they left town the next morning, the Mundis stopped at Café Paradiso, a local coffee bar, which had a reputation as a "hip" place. Though attempts had been made to contact the owners, no one had responded, so the chorus sang a few songs impromptu to a mildly interested audience. Lisa comments, "It was not in our mission to get in people's faces, but we definitely wanted to raise awareness and create some conversation. We sang songs like 'Something Inside So Strong' to help people understand us more."

On the way to Klamath Falls, the bus stopped at Chemult for lunch. 1998 Chemult was a tiny unincorporated community of about eighty people on Highway 97. There were a few stores and a gas station on either side of the road, a perfect place to stretch legs and grab a bite. All the women poured out of the bus to explore. Lisa remembers a couple of people going to a convenience store. "The person at the counter gave them the once over but was relaxed about the visitors. Then more women entered, and the cashier looked out the window at all these women walking around the community. The residents were obviously wondering what was going on and where had all these people come from?" Linda added, "That little town didn't know what hit it."

The tour group rolled into Klamath Falls around 3:30 p.m. and were directed to the Grange Hall. The time in Klamath Falls was by far the most memorable for many of the Mundis. A group of local residents had organized a community dinner to welcome the chorus before their performance at the Friends' Church. As the bus pulled into the Grange Hall parking lot, people looked out the windows at several butch-looking women with arms loaded with food. Pat remembers, "As we pulled up, there were all these women carrying pies and food trays into the hall. It was quite touching."

Inside, the long central serving table had every carbohydrate imaginable, along with meats, potato dishes, casseroles, and desserts. There was a turkey and pans of mac and cheese, as this definitely was not a Eugene potluck! Linda adds, "There wasn't a vegetable in sight. We called it the brown and white feast." Everyone ate heartily, as the food was wonderful, and any initial hesitance was soon forgotten. After dinner there was an open mike for anyone to perform, but there were no takers except for a few people telling jokes.

By the time the chorus arrived at the church, some were experiencing a "food coma." When they started warming up, it was clear people were having problems, since lots of carbs and breathing to sing don't work well together. Once the concert began, the audience didn't seem to notice any problems, since they kept looking around to see who was there. Lisa says, "We'd put up our risers on this rickety stage, and when we took our places, people bumped their heads on the overhang. We knew it wouldn't be a huge audience, but it was almost like there was no audience during the first set. They were trying to catch glimpses of who else had come in. It was all they were thinking about. There were like two people paying attention to us."

One Mundi adds, "They had spread themselves out and spent most of the time during the first half of the show craning their necks to see who else was in attendance." Lisa recalls the change at intermission. "It was like the endorphins after a massage. They couldn't contain themselves. After intermission, they all moved next to each other and everyone was present. Then it was a concert." The song "Cashmere Sweater" was a particular hit. Linda donned a hat and a tool belt and sashayed in front of the chorus while singing.

Everyone remembers two particular women, goat farmers, who had come down the mountain especially for the concert. They spoke of their isolation and how they had never publicly been out or around a group of lesbians. They were thrilled to be there, so much that they followed the chorus to the church service the next morning and to the concert in Roseburg two days later, since they had to go home and take care of their animals before traveling again.

Instead of checking into another motel, the Klamath

Falls community had planned homestays for the chorus. One of the hosts had organized an afterparty that most Mundis attended, and everyone, chorus members and community members, danced late into the evening. One Mundi recalls, "We stayed with the woman who owned that house, and she had sent her husband away—so her girlfriend could be there. We realized several women were in the same situation. It was like going back in time." Lisa adds, "I remember a long dance line moving through that large house and everyone singing 'I Will Survive' at the top of their lungs."

Some people slept well into the morning at their homestays, recovering from the night, but others were up at dawn for a visit to the wildlife refuge to watch the flocks of migrating snow geese. Then there was a morning church service before the group left. The minister had invited the chorus to sing, but there were very few people in attendance, although the goat farmers were there. Many in the congregation had boycotted the service. Undeterred, the minister preached about inclusion.

Pat adds, "Being in Klamath was initially eerie. They needed us. The OCA was visibly there, but there weren't any rallies or allies for support. In Eugene there was the OCA, but there was also a community of allies to fall back on. Not so for Klamath." For this reason, the tour bus stopped off at the downtown OCA office to sing to them before leaving town. They chose a defiant version of "Something Inside so Strong."

The chorus's next stop was Ashland, home of the Oregon Shakespearean Festival. Ashland is a cultural hub in Oregon with a strong LGBTQ+ community. The chorus was working with the Abdill-Ellis Community Center, built to commemorate two Medford, Oregon, lesbians who were murdered in 1995, and Women with Wings, the local women's choral group. When they arrived, the chorus visited the new community center where they were served lunch, miso soup and green salad—a cultural difference from Klamath!

Many Mundis spent a few hours exploring downtown Ashland. Then they arrived at the Congregational Church for their evening performance, splitting the program with Women with Wings, a more traditional women's chorus. Despite this difference in approach to music, they were very supportive in the collaboration with Soromundi.

The final stop on the tour was Roseburg, with a performance at the Roseburg Unitarian Universalist Church. One of the funniest moments of the entire tour occurred as Mac pulled the bus into the parking lot. It seemed that Daphne's absence had made her partner Judith's heart grow fonder, and she was there as soon as the bus hit town. Judith strutted up to the bus in full leather regalia. When Daphne looked through the window and saw her leather-clad spouse, she lifted her shirt and flashed her while everyone laughed and rolled their eyes.

The chorus enjoyed a potluck in the basement before the final performance. One of the goals of the tour was to perform and bring community together. Another goal was to encourage local voices in the community. To this end, the chorus preferred grassroots gatherings like potlucks and arranged "open mikes" before each concert where local women could perform. This was successful in Roseburg, though not so much in Klamath where there had been some reluctance to do this. The Roseburg group was much more comfortable, and a small bluegrass group sang as well as others.

Touring, especially for those not used to it, is both tiring and nerve wracking, even for professional groups. So, although most people had wonderful memories and experiences of the tour, that was not so for all. After the community potluck and open mike, one Mundi had a breakdown, becoming very agitated and upset. Pat, as a mental health counselor, deescalated the situation, and another Mundi arranged a ride back to Eugene once the situation was stabilized. Other Mundis prepared for the concert unaware of what was happening. Linda comments, "This is why for the 2013 tour, we literally labeled Pat the resident therapist."

Soromundi always draws a crowd in Roseburg—and sometimes protesters. Even though the overall community is conservative, there is a strong lesbian community there and several womyn's land compounds in the surrounding area. Still many women felt at odds with others in their larger community. Tour members appreciated this difference. As Pat says, "They were living more radically than we on the bus were. They've had to face a different environment."

As an acknowledgement of this different environment and to deflect it by poking fun, one of the songs on tour was "Go On, Mabon," directed at the OCA founder Lon Mabon. It was a rewrite of "Steal Away," and began with the lines, "Go on, Mabon, take your fear somewhere else!" It was sung with gusto and met with much appreciation.

Post-tour reflections were incredibly positive. Lisa still has artifacts, including some of Marty's handmade purple risers, now acting as amp stands, and her own hand-drawn program illustrations. Present Soromundi members who were on the tour recollect happy memories including one of Mac, the bus driver, attending the chorus's spring concert that year. The chorus had presented him with a Soromundi T-shirt, which he wore when he came up on stage to sing with them during an encore.

What has remained in people's memories were the different feelings about each place, the reception in each community, and the importance of our presence there. It was also important for the development of the chorus. Lisa states, "The group didn't give me very much trust until after the tour. I had to earn it. They realized if we trust the leader, we accomplish more. When we got back, the vision started shifting from those specific communities to the general question, How can we get out there? More people need us out in the world."

That epiphany, combined with the trust the chorus now had in Lisa, led to another major milestone—and Karm's return to Soromundi.

FIVE

fter the tour, Lisa was convinced that the chorus was not the same as it was when Karm had left four years before. "Karm and I bring different things to the chorus. I bring the technical, and Karm brings something magical. I wanted to resurrect that magic, but first I needed to test the group and make sure the trust was really there."

Lisa decided to have the chorus engage in some trust exercises. First, she invited some guests to work with the group—a singing coach from Lane Community College (LCC) for voice building and Dr. Ann Tedards from the U of O to work on classical voice technique. Tim Njoora, a music student from Kenya studying at the U of O, taught the chorus some music from his culture. Then Lisa added a song to the repertoire that was controversial: a campy version of Joan Jett's, "I Hate Myself for Loving You." She asked the group to wear sunglasses to achieve the appropriate rock 'n roll look and attitude. She knew that if the chorus could willingly perform a song about self-loathing, they were relaxing their political correctness. She hoped Karm would see that trust in the musical leadership existed. "I wanted Karm to know the group was very different and be assured of that."

Lisa asked Karm to return as a guest conductor for the song "Oh, Freedom" at the concert on May 30th, 1998, at Studio One in the Hult Center. The collaboration was successful, and the group expressed their appreciation for Karm, the founder of the chorus. At that point, Lisa began a dialogue with her, encouraging her to come back. "I told her, 'This group would be better with you here.'"

"I decided to give it a try," Karm says, and she rejoined for the 98-99 season. "I knew some of the people...but I was nervous, and excited, and anxious, and honored. I was vulnerable. It didn't help that my dad had died a few weeks before my return. After I'd been back for a while and people felt comfortable around me, women would come up to me and say, 'The chorus saved my life.' One woman in the bass section said to me, 'You'll never know what this has done for me. I come to chorus to save myself, and I commute from Albany.'"

Over the next few years Karm started to direct more and more pieces. "Lisa gradually lured me back to the podium."

They worked collaboratively for the next eight years. They became co-directors in season seventeen and the chorus benefited from their very different, but complementary styles. Karm described herself as a director who "flailed about." She possessed charisma and ideas to motivate the chorus. Lisa, on the other hand, had the formal education and musical training that ensured the chorus made musical progress. "I was in the teacher role, and Karm was amazing at the front role. She could talk to audiences, represent the group, and be our public face."

As the two reflect on the past, it's clear their different leadership styles balanced each other. This balance is easily obvious to the Mundis. According to Rebecca, "Lisa made us better singers and Karm was the energy." While Karm finds the joy in singing and rehearsing each week, Lisa often looks ahead to performance goals, imagining new events and creating ways to enhance the concerts in the future. They also took on different roles, with Karm taking the lead with the board and organization, while Lisa focused more on sequencing rehearsals and arranging music. Lisa often contributed her vision of what the choir could do, and the board would develop and update a five-year plan to accomplish that. Some of these goals required a lot of work, so easier years and productions would be scheduled in between years that would take a lot of time and energy.

Lisa admits, "Every time I came up with a crazy notion, Karm would say, 'Here are five reasons why that probably won't work.' Then we compromised, and instead of three people dropping from the ceiling, I only got one," she laughs. The "drop from the ceiling" was a trapeze artist descending and twirling in a hoop during the 2015 concert that featured *Adiemus: Songs of Sanctuary*, performed with an orchestra and dance troupe that entered in full costume down the aisles.

Karm adds, "I used to think every chorus needs a Lisa and every chorus needs a Karm. And that was just the beauty of our teamwork. There must be a visionary, and if it had been left to me, we would've just been rehearsing. Over the years, we've developed a license with each other, a permission to reign in the other."

Coinciding with Karm's return for the 98-99 season, was the birth of the *Sentimental Journey* CD. After the Oregon Tour, Lisa was convinced the group was ready to make a permanent imprint on the world of lesbian music, and she began planning the CD project. Prior to the tour, Soromundi had sung at First Presbyterian Church in Cottage Grove at the request of a pastor, Jamie Sparr, the first "out" clergy person in the Presbyterian church. Reverend Sparr was touring the country and speaking to congregations about acceptance and diversity. Some of the choir chose not to sing because the idea of singing at a regular Christian church service was traumatic. Also, half of the congregation didn't show up the day Soromundi sang, but Lisa and the chorus were impressed by both Rev. Sparr and the exceptional acoustics in the church. When it came time to find a location to record the CD, Lisa made a pitch to the church's board of directors to allow Soromundi to record in their sanctuary.

"Then I received a phone call from a member of the board," Lisa remembers. "He said the church board had a question, but he struggled to ask it outright. I waited him out, and finally he blurted, 'How do you recruit?' I automatically responded, 'Recruitment is only in September.' There was this dead silence, and I finally got what he was asking," she laughs. "They were asking if we, as lesbians, were planning to turn members of the congregation gay. I explained that it doesn't work that way. We had never—and would never—try to change a person's sexual orientation. I also emphasized that we only wanted to use the church at a time when no one was there, and we'd be recording into the late evening. We talked a little more. I explained we encouraged people to be themselves. When he called me again, he said the board was okay with it."

From a present-day vantage point, Lisa acknowledges the inconsistent quality of the CD, but she also recognizes it was a push forward into the future. "Parts of it are punishing to listen to, but it represents our process and growth. The teacher part of me wanted to hang in there and bring the group along and see where we could go and see if we couldn't make this into something more." Some of the flaws in that first recording were due to the chorus's musical ability, the location —despite excellent acoustics—lack of proper working equipment, and inexperience. But even with the flaws, Lisa quickly adds, "The heart and commitment of the chorus still shines through."

Karm summarizes her return and this time span by saying,

"Lisa calls this period the 'When We Got Back Together' period, and it touches my heart. We've weathered a lot, and I'm very thankful for that. Bridges weren't burned and everybody was forgiving and gracious...all for the good of the chorus."

Together Karm and Lisa would produce many memorable spring productions in the Soreng Theater. Their balanced strengths of musical training, creative production, and inspiring the choir translated into entertaining, worthwhile shows that established a faithful following who attends each year. The Mundis also have their favorite shows and songs that are routinely mentioned in conversations of the past.

The 20th Anniversary concert (2009) was the very first concert that involved extensive production. For prior concerts, the chorus mostly stood on risers and sang. Lisa worked with Carol Horne Dennis, a local theater director, to stage the show. Carol, along with her partner, alto Amber Lunch Dennis, wrote dialogue that would celebrate the group's twenty years. The first act began with three people seated in a living room at the side of the stage, two veterans and a newbie. The veterans use the scene to explain the history, beginning in Karm's living room. Then a small group representing the first chorus members came onstage and sang "Blackbird," while more Mundis entered, joining the song to illustrate the chorus's growth. The entire first act shifts between the Mundis in the living room, guiding the history forward, and the chorus on the stage singing songs that reflected specific moments of the twenty years.

At the end of the first act, the veterans present the newbie with a T-shirt. At one point, the sitting mayor, Kitty Piercy, appeared onstage to introduce "Ella's Song," a callout to young activists to keep protesting and speaking out, as Soromundi had done throughout its twenty years. This concert, or rather, production, was so incredibly different from past spring concerts that it made an indelible mark on the memories of Mundis and audience members alike.

Terra Omnis (2012) was an original work by noted local composer and arranger Audrey Snyder. Audrey had assisted the chorus at other times by critiquing arrangements or providing feedback at retreats. Soromundi commissioned this work to celebrate its twenty-third season and performed it in collaboration with the Denbaya Drum and Dance troupe. During this time, Soromundi had set goals of collaboration with local musicians and dancers, as well as broadening the types of music the chorus performed. The whole six-movement work celebrated the large continental land masses and oceans of the earth, an appropriate choral subject for the "Sisters of the World." Each movement had a different style and feel. Since the meaning of Terra Omnis is "the whole earth," it was fitting to evoke sounds from around the globe and pulsating drum rhythms. The drum troupe joined in three of the six movements, and the dancers celebrated different styles of dance and costuming for four movements.

Adiemus, *Songs of Sanctuary* (2015), a suite of nine pieces by Karl Jenkins, was the second act of the 25th Anniversary concert. Soromundi first attempted this work in 2002, after learning one movement at a time. By learning each song gradually over many performances and several years, assembling the entire set of nine pieces, while still challenging, made it possible for the non-audition chorus. Each piece is written in an invented language that is intended to be sung phonetically, with voices acting as musical instruments rather than conveying textual meaning. Building this performance was incredibly taxing, as no Mundi could rely on any previous native or foreign language they might know to make linguistic connections. Of course, as the Soromundi roster constantly changed, new folk had to rely on their peers for support.

Lisa remembers this progression. "During the Oregon

Tour in 1998, Linda slipped me a CD and asked me to take a listen. It was amazing and very accessible, not that hard. However, this was completely different than anything we had tried with the group. I decided to introduce one movement to see if we could help the group feel successful with it. We'd also just bought some Ugandan drums from a visiting choir, but that's a different story," she laughs.

"The year after the tour, we learned another piece, "Tintinnabulum," and performed it at the Gay and Lesbian Association of Choruses (GALA) Leadership Conference. It went so well that we started to pick up momentum and built support for the whole project. Overall, it was very calculated." She adds, "We were also worried about our audience and what they would think, so we developed a story map and included it in the 2002 program. One creative person drew different styles of footwear for each piece."

At the 25th Anniversary, the audience heard and saw the entire piece as both a visual and audial spectacle. Lisa notes, "This was the first time the entire suite of music was performed with an orchestra, a percussion ensemble, and dancers." The orchestra was Orchestra Next, a training orchestra in residence with the Eugene Ballet. It includes professional players as well as younger players gaining performance opportunities. In addition, six members of the U of O percussion ensemble were hired to play the difficult percussion score. The Denbaya Dancers returned to add movement to the individual pieces. The most memorable moment and the greatest spectacle was the trapeze artist (a member of the dance troupe) who descended from the ceiling in a hoop during one of the songs and performed a routine, challenging the chorus to watch the director and keep singing. This show is affectionately referred to by Mundis as "Cirque de Soromundi."

Adiemus, Songs of Sanctuary remains one of the greatest accomplishments for the non-audition chorus. If great reward is truly commensurate with hard work, *Adiemus* is Soromundi's proof of that truth.

Broadway (2017) is the most frequently mentioned Mundi favorite. What singer doesn't love Broadway? It was the first time costumes were extensively employed, such as the many costumes for *The Rocky Horror Picture Show* numbers. It was also the first time the chorus learned choreography from a professional dancer—a Mundi—the late Rita Monasterio. She added choreography and staging to songs from *Kinky Boots* and *Fun Home,* as well as pieces from brand new shows, *Hamilton and Hadestown.* These elements, plus a string quartet, brass quartet, and additional musicians, added theatrical nuance and drama to each song. The show was sold out, and its success opened the door for "Return to Broadway" in 2024 —another success and near sellout.

This ongoing exploration of themes, lighting, instrumentation, movement, and guest performers all in the name of entertaining the audiences, keeps the Soromundi fans coming back, wondering what else will Soromundi attempt? Each year, some in that spring audience are impressed enough to show up the following September and join the chorus. As for the veteran Mundis, those who return appreciate new ideas and challenges that keep the chorus program fresh and lead to further remarkable memories.

Six

undi Becky Bailey states, "Soromundi is fifty-one percent community and forty-nine percent music." Most veteran chorus members would agree that community is the heart of the organization. Long after a Mundi retires or steps away from Soromundi Lesbian Chorus of Eugene, the Soromundi community is still there for them, if they want it to be. For some, the community of women is the primary reason for joining the choir, while others are more interested in singing and performing.

Each person who walks into their first rehearsal has a different set of expectations and needs, but most have seen the group and have experienced the range of music and the sense of community that is immediately present. As new members join, they begin to understand how important this is. Becky adds, "When I was bass section leader, I would tell the new people not to worry about a stressful rehearsal. We'd go out for a beer later."

While many still go out for a beverage after rehearsal, in the early years, at a time when the gay and lesbian community was challenged and fighting for its rights, the choir community represented safety, acceptance, and relief from the outside world. Consequently, Mundis planned a multitude of events, and for some, the social committee was more important than the organizational leadership.

Lisa explains, "At the beginning we were building social cohesion, and it was important to build trust, so we had the group do things together. There was a Halloween Dance, a Masquerade Ball, some Valentine's Day dances, picnics, and the Prom You Never Went To." These events didn't simply meet social needs, but they also allowed women to pool resources, form work groups, share skills, and encourage or support one another.

Traditions were born—a welcoming picnic for new members, summer camping trips, regular poker nights, choir retreats, and a spring concert after-party. At many get-togethers, "downtime" often included members taking turns entertaining each other around the circle—reciting a poem, teaching or singing a song. One time a Mundi asked another to speak French for two minutes. Eventually the board engaged in a discussion and Mundi Barb suggested the choir do something just for themselves. Thus, the long-standing Tiny Talent Show, an annual showcase *for* the membership, staged *by* the membership, was born. The acts include the expected singing and playing of instruments, poetry, dance, as well as satirical sketches, dramatic readings, puppet shows, and outrageous, bawdy humor. As with Song Selection, the process where Mundis choose the upcoming repertoire, everyone knows, "What happens at Tiny Talent, stays at Tiny Talent."

Activities have always been organized outside of rehearsal because Lisa held—and still holds—rehearsal time as singularly focused on learning the music, only allowing a short break in the middle of the two-hour rehearsal. She is especially mindful of the Mundis traveling from distant communities like Roseburg, Albany, or even Portland. Each Tuesday their time investment is double that of the Eugene/Springfield Mundis.

The serious focus during rehearsal has sent the message that while auditions are not required, the chorus strives for continuous improvement and performance at the highest professional level possible. Songs are committed to memory, and very few hold music during the performance. Section leaders take attendance and schedule additional section practice ("sectionals") that help everyone learn the music. New members who cannot or will not meet the expectations set for performances often self-select out, but sometimes Lisa intervenes. "Years ago, there was a group of young women who arrived in September, our month to accept new members, but it was clear they weren't interested in anything but meeting women. Rather than asking them to leave, I gave the chorus a challenging song, and the altos [their section] a very difficult part. It was 'The Hammond Song,' by the Roches, and rather than try to meet the challenge, they dropped out."

It's very rare for Lisa or Karm to nudge people toward the door, and in fact, only two have been asked to leave in thirty-five years. Furthermore, there's a difference between those who are not in chorus for the right reasons and members who have a legitimate issue about the chorus or a song in Soromundi's repertoire. It is always permissible—and encouraged—for a Mundi to step out if she/they disagrees with a song's lyrics or message. Several Mundis have knelt in silent protest when Soromundi performed "The National Anthem" in concert, while others have stepped aside because a song has religious overtones that made them uncomfortable. Sometimes discussion opportunities are set up for members to comment or share opinions about lyrics and these conversations help some Mundis frame the concern from a new perspective. Ironically, some have acknowledged that although they shun the idea of singing "God songs," the Soromundi rehearsal is like church for them. One Mundi explains, "I come here once a week, see (and hug) my peeps, and we spend two hours collectively raising our voices in song." To that point, a local church choir director sent a card thanking Soromundi for their "ministry in music," after seeing them perform during her church service.

Soromundi is unique in that chorus retreats are more than just musical education. They are key to Lisa's plans to bring different perspectives to the chorus. "You know, in a typical performing group, the director's role is musical and artistic, and anything that you do in retreats is focused only to those ends, but I've always felt my job was more than music. I felt like I needed to do things that ensured the health and well-being of the group. And sometimes that means developing a better sense of community. Because if we care for one another, then we aren't going to have as much inner strife. We're going to learn to trust each other if we build that community."

Within the first few years of Soromundi, as word spread about the non-audition chorus whose membership was strictly female, it was inevitable that women who didn't iden-tify as lesbians would join the chorus. Women of varied orien-tations and identities found their way to rehearsal, loved singing, and relished the sense of community. Their arrival generated mixed feelings over the years—if they made their orientation known. Some Mundis welcomed the arrival of straight and bisexual women, celebrating a diversity of orienta-tions, others did not.

While most Mundis remember this disapproval spoken only in whispers amongst like-minded people, there were some overt comments that had to be addressed by leadership. Often, it was the passive aggressive behavior behind people's backs that caused the trouble. For a long time, some held to the belief that the name was Soromundi *Lesbian* Chorus of Eugene, and lesbians should be the *only* members—end of discussion. As more time passed, though, fewer and fewer Mundis clung to that outdated idea. They had first-hand experience with misogyny and discrimination and wouldn't consider judging others for their differences, so they welcomed these feminist allies.

Unfortunately, many lesbians were still hurting from the physical and psychological violence endured during the OCA years. Some Mundis thought straight and bisexual women shouldn't be allowed in the space since they had not experienced homophobia, nor did they face the comments and whispers each day at their jobs or out in the Eugene community. Linda remembers, "A good friend talked about how she wasn't going to oppose it, but she didn't like that straight women could come into this space. They had the benefit of being out in the world as a straight woman, and then they came into our space and enjoyed the female community."

Lisa states, "It was a difficult issue back in those days because it was very freeing and supportive to be in a lesbian-only space. But everyone needs that support and acceptance, so why wouldn't we build a larger community? At some point we'd said this isn't exclusively lesbian. I had to have a heart-to-heart conversation with certain members because they would say things that were driving women away. As a group, we said we were welcoming, but yet new members felt they couldn't be themselves. When one woman asked me what to do, I told her, 'Please help us. Please be yourself and let others deal with their own shit.'"

Lisa and Karm's support, along with the addition of some very strong women who would advocate for themselves, helped turn the tide. They had made it clear they wanted to sing under the banner, "Lesbian Chorus of Eugene," although they were not lesbians. These women wouldn't stand for the little comments and whispers. One straight Mundi, Anne Eagle, called people out and got involved in leadership. It should be noted that sometimes these straight women also experienced homophobia from their own family members, who questioned their sexuality because of their decision to sing in the "lesbian chorus." While many in the chorus have never had an issue with a person's sexuality, time eventually brought the rest of the chorus along, once they knew the women personally.

While Mundis slowly shifted their viewpoint about straight and bi women, embracing trans women, or supporting women as they transitioned to men, continued to be challenging. One veteran Mundi comments, "A trans woman cannot understand my experiences in the same way a lesbian can." While some hold this belief that "lesbian space" is the preference, most Mundis support the inclusion of trans women. However, what to do with female Mundis who transitioned to male has been a harder question.

Some Mundis who transitioned from female to male simply left the chorus during their transition. The reaction to their change was mixed. Jesse, one of the first Mundis who transitioned to male, helped educate the group by openly talking about their situation. Rob was still identifying as a woman when he joined the chorus, but as his transition progressed, the feelings about his participation diverged. Rob recalls, "Most people were very accepting of me as I transitioned; however, there were some difficult people. They weren't accepting and sometimes rude." Some of the Mundis wanted to make an exception for Rob and allow him to remain in the chorus. He states, "It was like, 'Well, it's Rob, so that's okay.' I wasn't sure if they'd have the same feeling if it was someone else."

As his transition progressed, Rob became a community Member-at-Large on the board. This was a new idea borne from the desire to keep Rob involved in some aspect of the chorus, but it was also an experiment to see if Soromundi would benefit from including a community member in its decision-making body. (Although the bylaws allowed community members to serve, the board had never utilized the opportunity.) By the end of Rob's service, it was realized that he presented a perspective that could not be duplicated by inviting a non-chorus member to the board. Kate comments, "We realized that since we're a working board, everyone must have knowledge of the chorus needs in order to serve. Rob's unique lens derived from his time in the chorus. That couldn't be achieved by someone who had never participated. Yet, it was still a great experience to have Rob's insights for the time he served."

Karm remembers, "We spent a whole year [2004] discussing whether to welcome the trans folks back and let them keep coming. One was a former leader of the chorus. From that discussion came the policy that Soromundi was for women-identified persons." This clarification helped to honor the grassroots heritage of the group, but it also discouraged some members who were considering transitioning from continuing to sing. Such is the ongoing struggle between being more inclusive and honoring the past.

Soromundi works to honor its legacy, recognizing that "women's space," is particularly important to those who have suffered trauma—some at the hands of men—and those who spend their professional lives in predominantly male-dominated professions. They find comfort and friendship surrounded by other Mundis. Harriet sums it up best and says, "For many, Soromundi is sanctuary."

While Karm had never specifically intended for Soromundi to become a women-only space, it was a natural byproduct of a lesbian chorus and became an unspoken rule without question for many years. She states, "I didn't come up with that. That came out of the membership. The headstrong ones in the chorus traditionally lobbied for a position they wanted, and lots of times, they got others to support them. The idea [that it was Karm's rule] was adopted."

Yet not all members believe the rehearsal space should be purely women's space. Over the years male choruses or mixed choirs have collaborated with Soromundi and come to rehearsals to practice together. Male musicians have been invited to play on Soromundi songs since 1997. "I remember riding to Roseburg with a younger Mundi, who was a separatist," Linda says. "At that time my son, Nick, was doing some drumming for Soromundi. The other Mundi was making the point that we shouldn't have boys [with the group]. I was shocked."

The debate of when and where there should be a "women's space" expanded to community activities. Can a woman bring her male friend to the Valentines Dance? What about a male child at a picnic? The rehearsal space had been claimed as "women's space," but was it realistic to tell a family they couldn't all be together in a public park? Such were the issues of the business meetings. Lisa states, "You can't just ignore fifty percent of the population [men], especially if you're at a family picnic or everyone is going bowling, and we've encouraged people to bring their partners." However, even when the choir policy was open and supportive, a few members were unhappy with the decisions and would choose not to attend.

Most Mundis are now perfectly comfortable with the presence of visiting male choral members from other choirs or male guests who are visiting at the invitation of a Mundi. Linda's experience from a few decades in the past is no longer the norm. However, there are still holdouts who find safety in women-only space, and whenever a situation arises that brings men into the space more frequently, the policy is tested.

Whereas the gender and sexual orientation questions were

raised multiple times over the years, no one thought to write a policy about age until a sixteen-year-old girl showed up and wanted to join. She appeared in September, the month Soromundi invites potential members to try out the chorus. Lisa recalls, "When we realized how young she was, we decided to have a meeting with her and her parents. The parents pushed hard. They were concerned that she didn't have support from people who knew what she was going through, and they really wanted us to let her join. This was long before there were Gay Straight Alliances (GSAs) in schools, so she really didn't have anywhere to turn. She was out and there was nowhere for her to be herself."

The situation forced the organization's leaders to reflect on the atmosphere, the musical content, and whether membership would be appropriate for a teenager. "At this point, we were still unfiltered and outrageous when we gathered," Lisa says. "It was a very relaxed atmosphere. We couldn't yet be ourselves and celebrate our sexuality in the mainstream world, so rehearsals could get bawdy. And this was long before anyone thought about what other choirs were like, let alone sexual harassment issues. We were very much into our own culture and having a good time." It was one thing to attend rehearsals and sing on a stage, but the community aspect of Soromundi was often rated "R."

The leadership recognized there would also be perception problems, as well as potential legal issues if Soromundi allowed a minor to attend rehearsals and fraternize at some of the more raucous, adult social events. As this was a time when the OCA was pushing the idea that homosexuality and pedophilia were related, critics could assert that Soromundi was "recruiting," a term often used by homophobes.

It was hard to say no to the teenager and her parents, and Soromundi tried to support her in her songwriting and singing. They encouraged her to perform at local coffee houses, went to her shows, and watched as she became a performer in her own right.

It's rare to have someone that young ask to join the chorus, and usually the youngest members are in their early to mid-twenties. Often these members only stay for a few years as they attend the U of O. One of Soromundi's newest members during the 23-24 season, Alanna, has played in various Soromundi concerts since she was fourteen. Her mother, Ruth, a longtime Soromundi member, offered her daughter a chance to play viola for certain songs when Lisa was putting together a string quartet. The experience was the road to her choice to become a Mundi.

As the chorus has matured, more and more experienced singers and musicians have joined Soromundi. This is a credit to the professionalism of the organization, the skill of the musical directors, and most importantly, the power of the community built by the Mundis.

As times have changed, the mainstream world has become more accepting of the LGBTQ+ community. As a result, some of the Soromundi-organized dances, poker nights, and other planned activities have waned in the last decade, especially during the era of Covid. However, the sense of community has not waned, but it has morphed into lifelong friendships for many. Sylvia remarks, "I'm an introvert, a home body. Soromundi gives me a community, people I can call to help me raise a shed, share vegetables with, and sing around a campfire. Soromundi gives me purpose."

There's a saying, "Once a Mundi, always a Mundi." Long after people step away from the rehearsing and performing, because of other commitments, family plans, or health, Soromundi is still part of their community, especially if they've nurtured relationships along the way. The Soromundi community leaves an indelible mark on most everyone who steps into the rehearsal space for at least a year, and there are

Mundis who have left an indelible mark on the organization. Joy Hainsworth was one such Mundi.

Joy lived in a big ranch house with beautiful old trees and horses out near Alvadore by the lake. She regularly hosted picnics, readings, and gatherings at her place. She had always been active in her church and advocated for senior rights as she aged. At one point, two of her fellow Mundis were grappling with transition. Joy learned one of them left the chorus because she didn't want to bring up the issue of "she" becoming a "he." Joy hosted a few discussion groups about being transgender, and she created a lending library so that people could come and check out books to understand more about the process. It was just how she was.

Lisa recalls, "I'll never forget when Joy was in her last week of life, and we all took off early from rehearsal to go visit her. I'd sent two people, Anne and Kay, ahead to figure out how we were going to do this. By the time we all drove out there, they had people with flashlights and safety vests on the road directing traffic and parking people in the field. Joy had been moved to the main floor of the farmhouse, where there were a few small rooms that adjoined the living room. We took over every room. People were standing everywhere singing...and we stayed and sang as long as we could."

Fifty-one percent community; forty-nine percent music. Sometimes at rehearsals, despite Lisa's focus on the music, that two percent from the community side permeates the whole environment. That happened on election night, 2016, when many Mundis showed solidarity with Hillary Clinton and wore pantsuits to rehearsal, confident about the election outcome. Chorus members couldn't stop checking the results as they practiced, and by the end of rehearsal, many were sad and crying, no longer able to sing.

Lisa says, "It's so important to remember that our chorus and rehearsal can be affected by anything that happens outside, like when a prominent local lesbian was hit, run over, and dragged by a car. There are also times when we learn about a past or present member who has died. There are moments when the life of the community is magnified and intensified because we all gathered, and we need to acknowledge those moments as a group. Sometimes there are great things to process—Obama's election, the defeat of Measure 9, the Supreme Court ruling on gay marriage—but sometimes there are horrific moments. It happens because we are so much more than a musical group. We're a family."

SEVEN

Gay and Lesbian Association of Choruses (GALA), grew from the individual community efforts in the '70s and '80s to establish queer choruses. With anchor choruses in San Francisco, New York City, Dallas, and elsewhere, a united network was formed. After forty-five years, GALA has greatly expanded with various programs and teaching experiences. GALA conducts leadership conferences, holds festivals, and supports the efforts of choruses in places like China. GALA now boasts hundreds of member choruses from all over the world.

From the beginning, Soromundi was interested in GALA; however, membership has been erratic since individual dues are out of reach for many, and it was unlikely that the chorus could ever afford to attend festivals, which are held in various locations throughout North America. The choir tried to lend its support to GALA by paying dues every other year, but plane tickets, hotel rooms, and registration for a chorus with sixty-plus members made the dream of attending and performing at a GALA event cost prohibitive.

These financial barriers were temporarily removed in the

early 2000s. From August 31st to September 3, 2001, Soromundi participated in the GALA Leadership Conference/Singers' Weekend in Portland. Not only was the financial aspect of the trip viable, but after a successful tour and CD, Lisa and Karm felt the chorus was ready.

Soromundi performed three unique pieces that evening: "Vichten," "Tintinnabulum," and "Circle Me Sisters." "Vichten," is a stylized and high-energy piece written in the style of an Arcadian folk song and utilizes a made-up language that imitates Mi'kmaq, an Indigenous language spoken in Canada and the northernmost areas of North America. "Tintinnabulum," a part of *Songs of Sanctuary*, the suite by Welsh composer Karl Jenkins, also utilizes an invented language, but has more of a Latin sound to which the chorus added drums. The final number was "Circle Me Sisters," a traditional folk song combined with a small group rendering of "Farther Along," a Southern gospel hymn. This piece begins with the chorus singing the folk song, followed by the small group with the gospel tune, and then both combine as the chorus sings "Circle Me Sisters" as a round behind the small group. This was a rousing and fitting piece to end Soromundi's unique and unprecedented performance.

In addition, Soromundi wore their colorful sarongs with varying patterns and symbols—that Lisa had bought at a yard sale. It should be noted that while the group refers to them as "sarongs," they were altered by the chorus to be ponchos, but the moniker stuck. Linda Cipriano remembers, "I got a call on a Saturday morning from Lisa. She asked if she could buy this stack of sarongs for costumes. We didn't yet have purchasing protocols in place, and they were only seventy-five dollars, so I said sure."

Many in the chorus thought the sarongs were too "feminine," though others appreciated the flowing style and vivid colors. Years later, long after the sarongs were retired, the

Mundis reflected and realized it probably hadn't been the best idea for a group of mostly white women to wear something that appeared tribal or from the Pacific Islands. The social justice movement helped everyone understand the difference between appreciating and appropriating another culture. But understandings were different in 2001. When Soromundi donned their sarongs at the GALA performance, they looked like no other group, sang songs that weren't choral, and their collective musical resume was thin compared to many of the other choirs at the conference. How would they be received?

As the authors of this memoir looked to document this seminal moment in Soromundi history, they could find few artifacts beyond the program and the memories of those who attended, and the memories lacked specifics, although most pointed to this singular performance as transformative. The entire experience could be distilled into one phrase shared by Anne Donahue. "GALA was a turning point for Lisa and for us."

Then, as the authors combed through the many boxes and folders provided by various Mundis, including Lisa, we found a lengthy reflection she had written in the early morning hours after Soromundi's performance. When we asked about the letter, she simply said, "I couldn't go to sleep. I just kept replaying it, so I had to write it down." What she wrote told the whole story.

Before we took the stage last night, I had hopes that it was the right time and place for Soromundi to emerge as a new and powerful force, but these were private thoughts, ones I hadn't even shared with those closest to me. I knew the venue was right, but I was uncertain about other factors, especially how the other choruses and their directors would play a role. Soromundi was ready and I knew by the second pickup rehearsal that we had a chance to create something—do something—that would take people by surprise.

I knew what the other choruses would be performing, and Karm and I agreed to show them something different. I also knew that some others would frown on the "folk" chorus elements — the lowered range, the choice in repertoire, the careful sidestepping of formal traditional skills. Still, Soromundi has come into its own and offers something much more valuable...the authenticity—the mystical, the experienced...the earthen, musical connection from heart and soul...if only we could capture that on stage tonight!

The curtain is up and we're beginning. The opening note is a little weak, but solid. We settle in and we're off. The intro [of "Vichten"] by Karen could not have been more perfect. Now the chorus is backing it up —very convincingly. Intonation, pace, pauses, style, diction, balance...this audience will be impressed with the first piece, and we'll be assured a good response, which will help with the next one. The chorus follows as I push the tempo and the tag is clean. Well done—and the audience responds as predicted, erupting into enthusiastic applause.

The second piece gets off to a great start. The chorus contains their energy, especially in light of the audience's response to the first piece. They set a mood with the chanting...and work the melodic line as it unfolds. The audience is relaxing halfway through the first run and by the repeat they're sighing. I can feel their reaction to the group and this piece—better than I expect— total acceptance of the non-traditional style and performance.

On the second time, though, the chorus must sense the audience's reaction and interest—either that or they're just relaxing... taking the lid off, expressing the line...feeling it together more than before. I look up to see them communicating with the audience; no director getting in the way here; just the raw emotion of this now-confident group traveling straight out into the room. The reaction and applause are excited, and I can see the chorus drawing energy for the third and final piece ["Circle Me"].

All of this energy...The anticipation is palpable as the stage shifts take place. The soloist, Daphne, begins...good contrast. The lines are working together...some stretching of the solo puts us slightly off the mark and I can't communicate with her...the chorus works/focuses to adjust and hangs in there. Altos save us with a rousing start to the round...good work. The chorus weaves the lines together and the tempo stays. The gospel group answers, and all are in top form. They move the tempo along as the chorus rejoins...We're home free!

Once again, the audience is uproarious and it is immediately clear that Soromundi won their hearts, seemingly unanimous. The chorus takes several bows —not smoothly—we really do need to practice this.

The festival directors are there to greet me after and congratulate me. It's appreciated and I try to focus, but I'm distracted by my upcoming role as emcee. When I walk on stage to the spotlight, I'm greeted with an overwhelming response from the audience. I'm forced to wait for a long while as the audience applauds. They applaud for Soromundi again, and in these moments, I hope the chorus members hear and understand what is happening. A man yells "diva!" and I'm forced to take a bow.

At intermission I'm mauled by the chorus's fans. No one passes by without introducing themselves and disclosing what Soromundi's performance did for them. Some are moved to tears... There are people that want to come to our future concerts... Two composers who want to work with us... A PR company from Portland offers help... Suggestions for more recordings. It's just more...more...more. We are all overwhelmed by this more-than-warm reception.

At the close of the concert, nothing could prepare me for the barrage of people that surround me to talk about Soromundi, the "premiere women's chorus in the West." People want to purchase my arrangements, fly me across country to work with their choruses... Directors and executive board members all want to *help us on a journey we have only considered in my head. It was like a crazy dream.*

Many Mundis remembered thinking on stage that things were going well. They could tell by Lisa's energy and the response by the audience. Barb, who was in the house for that performance states, "I was sitting next to two gay men who were going crazy during 'Vichten.'" The enormous applause at the end of the song stoked the chorus for the second and third pieces.

Perhaps the most appreciated characteristic by this audience of singers and musicians was the fact that Soromundi was a non-audition chorus, and yet the sound, the arrangements, and the performance seemed professional. Since these individuals understood that it was the director who was responsible for what happened on the stage, they celebrated Lisa throughout the event.

Pat states, "From the view I had, she [Lisa] was the star. All these other directors came up to her. We didn't sound choral and that was refreshing. Other directors asked, 'How do you do that?' People praised her and wanted to know things from her. It was a remarkable response."

In fact, as she mentioned in her reflection, Lisa was asked to fill in as the emcee and introduce other groups. Every time she reappeared on stage, she got a standing ovation.

The Mundis also basked in the performance glow. Sylvia remembers, "There were only about thirty of us and we knocked it out of the park. The audience gave us a standing ovation. We'd shed our sarongs after our performance, but we quickly put them back on as people were overjoyed and super complimentary."

Most veteran Mundis view the GALA performance as a highlight of their experience in the chorus. Kate recalls, "The chorus recognized it for what it was. That people who knew music actually thought we were good."

Eight

Soromundi's dues and collection system—a coffee can —made new Mundi Moke Varner uncomfortable. A bookkeeper by day, Moke recalls her discomfort. "When I joined in 2004, a coffee can sat at the front table and people dropped their dues into it. There was no receipt, no accountability, no knowledge of who paid and what they paid. We had no way of knowing if someone was struggling financially and might need help."

At the time, tracking dues was not a top priority; the choir had always functioned on the honor system and members assumed personal responsibility. Eventually chorus treasurers like Rebecca Swing and Jeanne Perry developed systematic ways that addressed these issues as part of the massive reorganization that was soon to occur. Moke would serve on the Finance Committee and introduce the idea of a "pledge card," which asked each member to commit to a dues amount they could afford. She also served as the cashier for many years, acting as the designated person who handles the deposits.

Soromundi has never hired professionals to manage the organization. Despite its numbers at times nearing one hundred, everyone is a volunteer—board members, section leaders, committee people. The music directors were originally volunteers, who might receive a little gift or bonus when the chorus could afford it. Now the Musical Director and Assistant Musical Director receive modest stipends since arranging music, organizing the productions, planning rehearsals, and assisting section leaders can be a time-consuming job. Also, as the artistic director, Lisa is the main contributor to visionary planning for the entire organization, offering project ideas, concert themes, possible collaborations, and grant ideas. When a task or project is outside the bailiwick of the membership, others are contracted for specific work such as tax preparation and website design.

Soromundi has always benefited—and suffered—from the strengths and challenges of volunteerism. While volunteers are uniquely invested and committed to the work of the organization, the tasks do not always align with a volunteer's skills, abilities, and time constraints.

Soromundi's organizational structure, which had begun organically as a grassroots group, was nearing another transition in the early 2000s. The names submitted as officers for the purposes of the non-profit, while definitely leaders, were not people viewed by the chorus as final decision makers. The *chorus*, following the consensus model, was the primary decision maker. The business meetings still were sometimes longer than the rehearsal, and in the effort to remain true to radical feminism, at times Soromundi got in its own way.

As the group continued to grow, the ongoing, regular work of the chorus relied on the same small group of people. Lisa describes this time as either "the same four people doing everything, or there were so many people on committees that they couldn't even find a meeting time."

By 2006, the musical directors and the organization were running on fumes. Lisa was exhausted and needed a break. "I needed to take a year off, and I thought we could find an interim director, but the organizational leaders said they were tired too. So it was agreed upon that we would all take a year and use it to reorganize. If I hadn't had the break...I know I was burning out. I had to plan all the events." Lisa acknowledged that everyone benefited from the one-year hiatus. Some members expressed concern that Lisa would leave permanently, but that was never Lisa's intention. She adds, "I knew I'd be totally excited to come back. I wasn't worried about my motivation for leaving."

Prior to the hiatus Mundi Jill Leininger was sent to a conference that focused on building sustainability for volunteer organizations. She returned with many good ideas, such as creating a new structure for the leadership. The hiatus allowed the chorus leadership to explore her findings. Furthermore, serendipity stepped in, and Rebecca crossed paths with a friend, Julie Weismann. Julie had spent years working as a consultant with non-profits, and the chorus committed to working with her to improve the organization. From her perspective, Soromundi was operating from a feminist consensus model from the past. "This model is okay, but it becomes exclusive. In order for it to work, everyone tends to become the same, and access isn't available for new people." Julie stressed that a formal structure provides a necessary framework. Organizations need rules and boundaries so new people know how to participate, and they can include themselves and not worry about fitting in.

Rebecca remembers, "Julie met with a small group of us a few times and talked about forming a board and the roles and skills needed." Memories of the chorus's work with Julie vary, but all agreed there were meetings with key organizational leaders and a large group meeting where members were introduced to the new structure of a board and encouraged to sign up for committees.

Julie asked Linda if she would be the first president and suggest other board members. Linda remembers, "I always felt I could be a president. Not on big boards, but I was president of my other choir. I knew we needed more structure, and boards are usually where you get that, yet nobody seemed to be in charge. I thought it was odd from the get-go. You need that lead person, the president."

As it turned out, the hiatus year happened at exactly the right time. Julie came to meetings and trained the new board who had time to become familiar with the new structure and engage in planning and capacity building for the future while Lisa gained time to rest and rejuvenate. That year of restructuring possibly saved the chorus.

During the year hiatus, Soromundi established a formal board, and Linda Cipriano became the first board president in the "Modern Era" of Soromundi. Karm adds, "Linda got in there and worked her tail off." Linda had been involved in the leadership ever since she joined ten years before, and the group trusted her.

By the end of the restructuring, Lisa and Karm were elated that they were only responsible for the music and production decisions—not logistics, not marketing, nor details like hiring and paying the American Sign Language (ASL) interpreter. They focused on the artistic and musical vision. It also gave the group momentum as they used the next year to prepare for the 20th year—and the next CD.

Some people had worried taking a year off would slow the chorus's momentum. Linda had no such fears. "I felt like we came out of the gate running. I heard people worried about the hiatus, but I don't think we missed a step, as a choir or organization."

Lisa was also anticipating a twentieth-year celebration. "We had this renewed energy. I knew we needed at least a year back before we go into our twentieth year, because we wanted to do something big. I now had enough energy for a CD and a celebration. The hiatus ended up being the smartest thing we've ever done, not only organizationally, but I think that it gave me a chance to reflect on what the group had become and its potential. I think that was the start of the 'mature period' choir."

Linda served for five years, stabilizing the new board structure, although there were still some long discussions and differences of opinion. One Mundi remembers, "Linda moved us from group consensus to board work and protocols." Linda describes this time as "just trying to find our footing and using any kind of management and leadership skills I had." She created a strong foundation of acceptance and trust that positioned the chorus for future organizational development and the leaders to come.

————

What happens when a lawyer (Pat Vallerand), a researcher (Cathy Thomas), and a Ph.D. (Jeanne Perry) join an unpretentious, energetic young president on the board? Just as Lisa had appeared in 1990 at exactly the right time to help Soromundi musically, President Amber Smith and the board of directors in 2012 weren't afraid to roll up their proverbial sleeves and grapple with the necessary requirements to create the policies, protocols, and structures that still exist today. Amber's skill set included listening, trust building, and learning—from a group of professional women with decades of experience in leadership. She was valued for her commitment to fairness and equity. Amber also represented the next generation of Soromundi leadership.

During Amber's tenure, the Non-Profit Clinic at the U of O's Law School provided an opportunity for Soromundi to have an assessment of their organizational structure. As Cathy explained, "We needed to really make things clean and clear and make sure that we were strategic about having policies and procedures. Finance needed to be cleaned up too. We needed to really instill checks and balances regarding our money handling. It was a perfect time because this was a way to evaluate what we'd started and work on where we still needed to be."

The assessment validated much of the chorus's work thus far and pointed out the steps it still needed to take, such as writing a mission statement, which was a far departure from Soromundi's radical roots.

As the organization developed, there was a need to make sure there was not a divergence between the musical vision and operations. As Co-Musical Director, Karm sat on the board as a non-voting member. Given the fast-growing chorus numbers, larger events, and more complicated productions, this was a necessary link. "It worked really well," Lisa recalls, "because Karm could keep me informed about what was going on, regarding the business side of the organization, and she could share the vision and offer the board information about our musical plans. Karm and I were very strategic in how we would all work together."

As liaison to the board, Karm was helpful in moving the organization forward. Cathy had been attending monthly talks organized by the Non-Profit Association of Oregon. "They had ten months of guest speakers on mission and values, strategic planning, and development." She and Karm then went to a conference focused on strategic planning, and they brought this information back to the board, which then spent almost a year clarifying the chorus values, creating a mission statement, and writing a strategic plan.

Karm reflects, "It was like, okay, we're mature, we're sustainable. You know, all the things that you envision the older it gets, the healthier an organization gets. Those things just felt like the next step." Lisa had been collecting anonymous feedback from the membership for many years, having members evaluate their musical experiences. The yearly feedback was expanded to include the board/organizational leadership. Lisa states, "We have always wanted to hear from our members about their experiences to keep the communication lines open and to tell me how I'm doing. It was only natural to expand this to include all aspects of the organization. It helps us (leaders) be accountable to the choir, and it helps us measure the health and cohesion of the group." The board invites Lisa to provide a quantitative and qualitative summary of this data in the summer board retreat, which continues today as the "Annual State of the Choir."

More steps followed from successive boards, including improving the use of technologies such as designating Dropbox as a place for official chorus records, creating a grievance policy, clarifying bylaws, and initiating board trainings. Most important, the musical vision and strategic planning became integrated. Many people played crucial roles in this ongoing development, including later boards under the presidencies of Kate Barry and Micki Varner, respectively.

Julie Weismann has said Soromundi is her example of the most sustainable, all-volunteer, non-profit in Oregon. While there are still areas where Soromundi needs to grow, it has achieved its status as a mature professional organization, one that still values its feminist foundation and commitment to member involvement.

NINE

Collaborating with musical groups and artists has been a part of Soromundi's history since the early days. In the third season, Ysaye Barnwell of Sweet Honey in the Rock visited and conducted a workshop with the chorus. There was also a drumming workshop during season five to help Mundis with their sense of rhythm and pulse. As the chorus gained momentum, it was time to reach out and share the stage. Lisa states, "The [1998] tour highlighted the need to support other communities."

Lisa and Karm developed an idea they named The Building Bridges Outreach Project. Karm wrote a grant and successfully received funding through the Equity Foundation that would bring the Soromundi experience to Roseburg, Bend, and Newport. Each event would feature local community members "joining the chorus" for a day. This involved local women coming to a daylong workshop with the chorus and singing several songs with them at a concert in the evening. These were complex events, involving detailed logistics, advanced planning, and sometimes arranging overnight lodging for the chorus.

The outreach involved extensive communication with local churches, civil rights organizations, and community centers to locate a large venue in the proposed city. Community members who were interested would fill out a registration form. Then came the production team and plans to handle both the chorus (*e.g.,* transportation, lodging, food, costumes) and the participants (*e.g.,* music packets, catering, concert logistics, and prep for rehearsals). During the day, games and singing exercises stressed the need to have fun and rely on each other. Participants later described it as "musical fellowship."

The concerts didn't attract large crowds but planted important seeds. After each event, participants evaluated the experience (a required grant condition) and made suggestions to improve the workshops. It was a huge effort but worth it for the extensive engagement with the communities involved. Linda, who was chorus president at that time, says, "For Building Bridges the most important thing was the community outreach. That was big and always a good experience."

Alongside the outreach projects, Soromundi has also worked throughout the years to promote community engagement locally. For several successive years Mundis performed a winter concert at LCC to benefit the Women in Transition Program, which supported women working to change their lives through education. The concerts also involved collaborations with other choruses, including In Accord, Confluence, and the Eugene Peace Choir. In 2011 the concert was combined with a "Be a Mundi for a Day" workshop, repeating the successful Building Bridges format for the local Eugene community. Some of the participants in that workshop became chorus members who are still Mundis today.

As Soromundi continued to grow, leadership scouted for a larger rehearsal location. Lisa wanted tiered seating, and they found the dilapidated North Eugene High School (NEHS) music room. While Soromundi could use the facility, it wasn't available for the school choir because of budget cuts. Through a collaboration among Soromundi, school administration, and the Pride Foundation, many Mundis participated in a work project facilitated by the late Chris Ashburn, a North Eugene parent and veteran Mundi. The work crews, organized by Sylvia Sandoz, renovated the room before the school's open house for prospective students.

"I came to paint because I had those opportunities as a kid," says Mundi Daryl. "I can't imagine my life without music education, and I want to give back so other kids learn to appreciate music." Mundi Mary Robertson still has a tangible reminder. "I put on my blue jacket one day and realized I still have a drip of cream-colored paint on my sleeve from painting the band room at North Eugene High School. I think Cathy was on some scaffolding and dripped on me as I stood underneath."

The Mundis time at NEHS and their interaction with students planted seeds for a future endeavor with young people—the "Be the Change" tour (also called The Northwest Tour). It was a difficult time for LGBTQ youth and the sobering statistics on youth suicide stirred the choir to action. During that tour, the chorus heard about Bridging Voices, a Portland youth choir built from members of Gay Straight Alliances (GSAs). Lisa remembers, "When we went to work with the youth groups up in the northwest, that's where we heard about the Portland youth choir, and we were thrilled when they decided to come down and spend the day with us."

In the months before the workshop, Kate, who was concerts chair at the time, visited GSAs in the local schools to encourage young people to attend. The idea was for local youth to come to the workshop, then attend a few rehearsals, and join the chorus at the spring Hult Center concert. A few did but as Lisa remembers, "We only had a small group that were able to come. It seemed that our outreach outside of town was more effective than in town." Local gay youth had fewer resources. Not all high schools had GSAs, and the membership was often small.

The Bridging Voices workshop was a great success. Their concert with the chorus was titled "Be the Future Now." Soromundi had T-shirts made with the title on the front and "Find your Voice, Sing Out, Change the World" on the back, a fitting slogan for the day. Students traveled down the I-5 corridor with parents and chaperones, who also joined in the fun. Throughout the day the young people shared their stories of adversity, hopes, and triumphs. Mundis supported, listened, and learned. Many of the youth told stories that reminded Mundis of their own past experiences, and as a result, they forged tight bonds with the students. Karm noted, "By the end there wasn't a dry eye in the house. It was a good day."

The Be the Change Tour and work with youth choruses highlighted an urgent need to support the trans community. Leadership also realized that more young members were identifying in new ways—non-binary, CIS—and adopting new pronouns. As a result, the leadership re-examined and expanded its own membership statement, and workshops and discussions were held at subsequent retreats.

The fall retreat in 2018 opened the door for the chorus to have a focused discussion about gender identity. The chorus was lucky enough to find Transpose PDX, a new Portland transgender and non-binary chorus. In March 2019, Soromundi invited Key of Q, a subgroup of Transpose PDX, to be part of a daylong workshop and joint evening concert. Key of Q was an acapella group of transgender, non-binary, questioning, and gender queer singers. Lisa met with their director, Ash, several times to create the content and activities that would allow the two choruses to learn from each other. Unlike other workshops, this day focused less on singing and more on sharing stories and discussing identities and meaning.

The small group of Portland singers arrived, somewhat nervous, as they had experienced some negativity when trying to sing with other gay-identified choruses in the past. They were reassured by a warm welcome. The two directors shared the sensitive content, following their plans to intentionally make mistakes and openly show how to correct and support one another. Even though the activities and discussion questions were mapped out in advance, there were still some tense moments, but the ensuing sharing of experiences was honest and emotional. The Mundis in attendance learned a lot about difference and new ways of thinking, even though there was still some ambivalence and hesitancy about potential changes to Soromundi's membership definition.

The evening concert affirmed everyone's appreciation for the Portland group. This small group of acapella singers performed with a spirit and musicality that went far beyond their numbers. Their beautiful sound captured the audience, many of whom may not have been exposed to such clear visual differences in gender expression. It was a testament to the power of music to foster acceptance and change.

Community outreach is commonly thought of as one group reaching out to another community with the aim of affecting change of viewpoint or understanding. Some of Soromundi's outreach efforts have followed that pattern. However, at its best, community outreach is a two-way street, producing change for both groups. Mundis gained as much from the outreach to youth and the Portland chorus as they offered in support and joint singing.

Lisa states, "We *always* learn more than we think. Every exposure to other choirs, other communities, and other directors helps us grow. It doesn't just affect our singing; it enriches our lives."

Not all of Soromundi's collaborations have been organized down to the last detail. In fact, one of the chorus's favorite memories involves a Russian dance troupe that just happened to be visiting Eugene.

In 2008 the chorus was told that a traveling Russian choir would be coming to a rehearsal. They were coming to Eugene as part of a Slavic festival organized by Ilana Ivashover (the owner of a local Russian restaurant) and others. Mary remembers, "When I came into rehearsal that night, instead of just a chorus, there were dancers and instrumentalists—all in colorful native costume. Most of us could not speak one another's language, although Karm and Yelena kept agreeing that 'vodka good'." The troupe taught the chorus "Kalinka," a Russian folk song, as well as a few Russian words and expressions and then danced and played for them.

Afterward there was conversation and sharing. The Mundis learned the troupe was not supported well, and they were nervous that their festival was not being publicized. Concerned that there would not be many people in attendance, Soromundi agreed to sing with them that night at Condon School, in the hopes of garnering more of an audience. The concert indeed had not been publicized, and there was an audience of two—Mary's sister and Mundi Dawn DeWolf's partner. So, the two groups simply performed for each other. Soromundi sang the first set to much applause from the Russian group, and the chorus was equally delighted by the Russians. As Mary described, "They performed traditional Russian songs and dances, strummed balalaikas (a triangular-shaped instrument similar to a guitar), and featured leaping Cossack dancers. Such amazing talent." When the Mundis stopped cheering, everyone joined together dancing, laughing, and singing. When collaborations such as these happen, the performers themselves are changed by the interactions they have. Who needs another audience when we have each other?

TEN

The first 1998 tour plus the runout concerts of Building Bridges built momentum for a tour that would connect with queer youth in different cities and raise money for the organizations that supported them. It was 2012, and the "It Gets Better" movement was rippling through the LGBTQ+ communities nationwide. GSAs were cropping up throughout the states, and for the first time, queer teens and their allies were coming together as a group with a caring, often queer adult advisor, who could serve as a mentor.

Lisa explains, "Everyone seemed to be aware of the high teen suicide rate, and we all wanted to help. Soromundi set its sights on supporting LGBTQ+ youth. Members of the group lent their voices, speaking in schools and churches, and producing videos to post online. And the leadership decided to take the chorus on the road to "spread the love."

It was a worthy goal, but Lisa recognized that many in the chorus would also benefit from some reflection around the issue of the "generation gap." Times were changing and many still held strong opinions about lesbian culture, not understanding new perspectives or what the Millennials faced. If the chorus interacted with the younger people, what the youth valued would be critical to forming trust between the two groups. Lisa realized the retreats prior to the tour would provide the opportunities to bridge this gap through her unconventional but very effective methods.

"Before the Northwest Tour, the two retreats prior moved us in that direction. I divided the chorus by age, and they were not happy campers," she remembers, laughing.

The Mundis had resisted being separated by age into discussion groups, answering questions like, "Do you feel safe expressing your identity/orientation? If so, where?" as well as "What would you tell your fourteen-year-old self?"

Lisa states, "The chorus let me run my sociological experiments on them because I was transparent about the goals, and we always shared the outcomes."

In the end, it proved to be a significant step toward understanding the much bigger picture. "We transcribed the notes from those meetings," Lisa explained. "When we shared the results, we saw that those over the age of fifty had completely different interests and perspectives than those under forty. And those from forty to fifty-five also had differing perspectives. We realized that to connect with the youth, we needed to be more open-minded, instead of focused on our own specific issues. It was really valuable."

The exercise taught many of the Mundis that they would be learners as well as teachers when engaging with the younger generation. Of course, they were also learning to be more open with each other.

The tour, titled "Be the Change," was also planned two years in advance. The tour committee, co-chaired by Kate and Barb Hilding, contacted representatives of the Oregon and Washington Pride Foundations respectively, who put them in touch with youth groups and organizations in several different northwest cities. They eventually settled on performances in three cities—Portland, Tacoma, and Seattle, from Wednesday April 17th to Sunday April 21st, 2013. Each performance was planned in conjunction with LGBTQ+ youth centers in the three communities. Lisa and the tour committee worked with the centers to ensure a strong interaction between the youth and the chorus.

At the next retreat, the chorus worked to craft and test discussion questions and definitions that would shape the content that would be shared with LGBTQ+ youth groups. The youth at these centers responded to questions about gay culture, changes for the gay community, their own experiences and sense of identity, and their plans and hopes for the future. As a result, some of the young people shared their perspectives by volunteering to introduce songs at the concerts.

The centers or their sponsors supported the tour by arranging venues at no charge. Costs were further mitigated when the chorus received a grant from the Equity Foundation. Most Mundis paid their own way, and some did fundraisers, such as bowl-a-thons.

As the chorus had already done a tour and several "run out" concerts around the state, their "travel savvy" was high, and every detail of Be the Change was meticulously planned. Cathy produced a daily itinerary covering every aspect of the multi-day journey. Kay headed up the riser and roadie crew, the tour committee made sure that all members were accounted for at all times, and three therapists were enlisted to offer support, but Pat served as the official "tour therapist," for anyone experiencing tour stress. A sign above her seat on the bus proclaimed, *The doctor is in!*

The chorus left that Wednesday from Valley River Center. There were two buses, each with its own personality. One had a lively group and it was quickly nicknamed "Rita's Party Bus," while the other one was quieter. Mundi Lindsay Bailey also lightened the journey by offering to streak people's hair with Soromundi purple. Everyone seemed to look after one another, such as the impromptu "help crew" for a wheelchair-using member, ensuring her full participation in the tour itinerary.

The first stop was the Cascade Campus of Portland Community College (PCC)—in NE Portland. Although the chorus had been assured that there was ample parking next to the performance venue, that turned out not to be the case, and the bus drivers had great difficulty accessing the spaces available. Kay, a bus driver in her day job, took charge immediately. She sprang up and maneuvered both buses into a space. Everyone dispersed for a quick pre-concert dinner, helped along by the nearby restaurant options researched by the tour committee. PCC donated the use of the hall, and proceeds from the concert benefitted the Sexual/Gender Minority Youth Resource Center (SMYRC) and PCC Rock Creek Queer Center. One young representative of the Queer Center introduced several of the songs, which was appreciated by both the chorus and the audience that included members of the Portland Gay Men's Chorus.

Immediately after this success, Mundis piled back into the buses to drive to Olympia for an overnight stay in a motel. Perhaps it should've been a sign of things to come when the bus pulled up at midnight and heard the fire alarm going off and saw the motel being evacuated. In the morning, some Mundis reported seeing bed bugs, sending panic through the group. However, by the time some returned from a morning trip to the wetlands, it was determined the critters were roaches. All part of the joys of touring. At least it provided a break before they were off to Tacoma.

One of the fondest memories from the Mundis interviewed occurred at their Tacoma concert spot—the Kilworth Memorial Chapel at the University of Puget Sound. Kilworth is notable for its history and its glorious pipe organ. Designed by renowned organ builder Paul Fritts, the organ was modeled after the great organs of the Baroque period. Its twenty-foot span of tiered silver pipes extended to the ceiling and the gold scrollwork provided the classical accent against the white woodwork. The bench and keyboard were hardly visible from across the room.

It was in front of this great organ that Soromundi would perform to raise money for Tacoma's Oasis Youth Center, which had an established youth and adult partnership, connecting them for "learning, teaching, and action." Many of the youth arrived to hear the chorus, taking their seats in the first two rows. Some Mundis remember that the kids at first seemed disengaged, paying more attention to their phones than anything else. Many in the chorus were, of course, old enough to be their parents or grandparents, and the teenagers' healthy dose of skepticism was obvious in their body language.

When the group opened with the relatively new song, "Price Tag" by Jessie J, the kids began to pay attention, especially when Mundis Emily and Pam stepped forward to do the rap verse. In addition to Lisa on the keyboard, Karm played bass, and Dani was on drums. It became clear this wasn't a usual "church" chorus. However, it would be the song "Creep" that transformed the concert. The 1992 Radiohead classic immediately grabbed the attention of the queer teens in attendance. Lisa's slower, intense arrangement along with the haunting background provided by the chorus, was the perfect backdrop for Emily's soft and almost tentative phrasing during her solo. When she achingly sang, "I'm a creep, I'm a weirdo," the change in the youth was noticeable.

Cathy remembers, "The kids reached for their phones and started texting. They were telling their friends to get to the concert."

"It was meaningful for all of us, too," Emily remarks. "The

song is so powerful and hearing the chorus behind me...It gives me goosebumps just thinking about it."

By the second half the whole youth group in the audience had doubled in size, everyone paying attention, laughing and mouthing the words to some of the songs. For the final song, "Keep Your Head Up," the chorus went down into the audience and lined the sides of the chapel as they sang. The chorus's confidence and the rapport with the audience is evident in the video on Soromundi's YouTube channel.

After the concert, the teens mobbed Emily as the chorus disassembled the drums and risers. Waiting for the buses, the chorus had time to marvel at the magnificent organ in the chapel. Organ maker Paul Fritts believed that we "hear with our eyes," when we see "an ornate and elaborate instrument" such as the Kilworth pipe organ. Lindsay, an accomplished pianist, got permission, and decided to try to play it. Lisa remembers, "So we're getting ready to leave, and Lindsay starts playing the organ. It was just silliness because she didn't know how to play the foot pedals. I crawled underneath to operate them as Lindsay played the keys." (This resulted in a very memorable and treasured chorus photo of Lisa flat on her stomach, butt in the air, with Lindsay at the keyboard.) It was a fun and silly moment after an emotionally charged performance. See the photo at: https://tinyurl.com/soromundibook.

Karm summarizes, "There was something magical in that Tacoma space." Indeed, everything came together that day for one of Soromundi's most treasured performances.

Another clear memory was the "Flash Mob" planned for the group's lunch break at the Southcenter Plaza in Tukwila, Washington. The food court, located on the second level, would be the center of the mob. Everyone got lunch and arranged themselves around or near the food court. Lisa remembers, "It was so fun because we all dispersed, and we had a tight timeline and signal for when we'd move in."

The mall administration and security were not notified, and Lisa warned the chorus they would need to leave immediately if security showed up. Then the roadie crew set up an amplifier on a rolling dolly, and Cathy did reconnaissance for a centrally located outlet. Once found, the roadie crew quietly hauled Lisa's keyboard into the mall. She adds, "We decided to disperse along the balcony area overlooking the first-floor escalators and stairway."

Pat recalls, "It was building up to the moment. Some of us felt like we were wandering around like spies, waiting for it to start."

Then, amidst the lunch rush, the first notes were played on the organ and Angie belted out the opening verse of "Let it Be," over the second-floor railing to the first floor. Marty comments, "She was so brave; she just started singing and everyone looked around to find her."

The other Mundis stopped, stood, and sung from wherever they were, slowly moving toward the food court as the momentum gathered. They removed any jackets and overshirts, revealing matching Soromundi T-shirts underneath. By the end of the song, the entire choir lined the balcony and the food court, singing the song's gospel-like chorus at the top of their lungs. The crowd was not sure what was happening at first, but once they caught on, they seemed delighted, and passersby congratulated the singers and took selfies with the choir members.

———

The last leg of the Be the Change Tour was Seattle. The Mundis had free time before the concert to explore and play tourist. Small groups headed to the aquarium, the piers, or the underground tour. The Seattle concert was held in an old Baptist church. Lisa remembers, "It was a difficult venue to get into because it was like a maze with many corridors and a tiny back staircase." It was tough for the roadie crew to haul equipment up about twenty stone steps. The concert was a joint performance with the Seattle Women's Chorus and Diverse Harmony, the gay/straight youth alliance who rehearsed in the church.

The Seattle Women's Chorus sang first. Karm appreciated their professionalism and noted, "They graciously allowed us to perform after them." Other Mundis noticed their more formal dress and approach to the event. "What was immediately obvious to me," Pat comments, "was the difference in attire. We were like lumberjacks in their bathroom." Kara adds, "I felt completely underdressed."

Lisa notes, "Their skill was obvious, and I was glad our choir got to hear them. There's so much to learn from such a polished, professional group."

The youth chorus was next. They were joyful and enthusiastic, performing some contemporary songs and jazz pieces. A favorite was an arrangement of the recently released "The Story" by Brandi Carlile.

Soromundi sang last and the audience response was amazing. Lisa recalls, "We sang well, and the audience was really engaged and impacted by the lyrics. It was just electric, and then we got to finish with 'Let It Be,' where great solos by Angie, Amy, and Karm always bring down the house. It was an immediate standing ovation. I imagined it like La Scala where they're throwing things at you, just out of exuberance. That's how it felt in the room." The concert ended with all three choirs singing together.

People yet again could not believe that Soromundi was a non-audition chorus, and chorus members were met and thanked by so many members of the audience that it took a very long time to get backstage and change. The Seattle Women's Chorus threw an after party in a local bar where many Mundis danced the night away.

The tour was a resounding success with tour members expressing that it felt important to reach out to youth. The ticket and CD sales allowed the chorus to donate over $3000 to the three youth groups who sponsored them. The tour built both connections and memories—and immense preparation for the rest of the season. Mundi Elizabeth said, "After five days of traveling and performing, the spring concert that year was a breeze!"

ELEVEN

It's 7:15 a.m. on a Saturday morning in early June. Sylvia Sandoz, Song Selection Coordinator for the chorus, inventories the supplies in her truck once more before she leaves her house, comparing the contents with her list for a second time. She had to make a quick run to an office supply store last night when she realized she was short two hundred stickers, which will be needed for voting. While home isn't far away, and she could run back if something crucial was missing, fifty-plus people would wait for her return, slowing down a process that already needs the entire day to complete.

Satisfied she's packed everything, she heads to the Longhouse at LCC. By nine a.m., sixty people, nearly two-thirds of the chorus, will assemble and participate in the last activity of the season: Song Selection, the event where the current Mundis select most of the music for the subsequent season. This is Sylvia's twenty-fourth year with Soromundi, and her twelfth as Song Selection Coordinator. She will readily admit that she's a much better musician than she is a singer, and if there were auditions to join Soromundi, she'd excel at reading music, but when it came time to sing, she'd struggle.

But this is Soromundi. There are no auditions. Although it is helpful, no experience or vocal training is required to join. Today the entire chorus is invited to help select next season's repertoire. All of those who can make a Saturday event will be there, including Mundis with extensive musical training and degrees as well as their fellow Mundis who love to sing, but may have little understanding of key signatures, music vocabulary, and arrangements.

What will happen today is the culmination of months of work—by Sylvia, the music committee, the music directors, and chorus members who submitted the songs that will be considered. The submission process was completed in April, and any current member could submit up to five songs, a number that varies from year to year. Submitters follow a one-page process that requires finding lyrics, obtaining an audio track of the song, and providing an English translation if the song is written in a foreign language. The chorus usually has a theme, and this year's theme is "Past and Present."

Between the submission due date and today, Sylvia has spent hours selecting audio clips that will be played and compiling lyrics into a booklet. The audio clips must represent the part of each song that will be considered—verse, chorus, bridge—as well as areas that represent the style and choral possibilities for arrangement. Then the music committee, the directors and sectional leaders, do a "first listen" to sort the songs into genres and ensure each song heard is possible to arrange. Very rarely does the committee decide a song is not in any way suitable for the chorus, and any disagreements about lyrics or genre are typically left for the whole group discussion. After that meeting, Sylvia uses feedback to adjust the clips and materials before copying the lyric booklets for each attendee.

A small group of Mundis is waiting at the door when Sylvia arrives. They are there early to set up the room. Before 9:00 a.m., they'll unfold dozens of chairs and tables and prep the buffet line for the catered lunch, while Sylvia organizes the supplies each Mundi will need for the tasks today—a scoring sheet, a pencil, and the booklet listing the lyrics of the seventy-two songs from the first listen. Other volunteers set up the sound system and prepare the butcher paper sheets that will go up on the wall to record the group's choices. Soon the Mundis trickle in and scout out places to sit. Some people bring camp chairs, snacks, and water bottles. Some have brought their knitting, giving their hands something to do while they listen to dozens of songs.

When 9:00 arrives, the facilitator, former President Amber Smith, establishes necessary ground rules, walks everyone through the day, and ends by stating the purpose. "For those of you who are new, this process might seem tedious, but it's also unique. I know of no other chorus where the membership selects the songs, where every single member gets an equal voice, equal to the directors' voice today."

For the next two hours, the room is almost completely silent as Amber introduces each song and the Mundi charged with running the audio plays its corresponding sixty-second clip that captures the essence of the song. Amber also reminds the group that each song is attached to someone in the room and criticism should be given with care. Offering up a favorite song for consideration and often receiving criticism is difficult, which is why it was decided years ago that the identity of the song proposer be anonymous. Members focus on the task, some taking extensive notes about instrumentation, number of words that will need to be learned, or how difficult the piece seems to be. Others go with what they feel and just rate the ones they really like.

At the short break, Mundis take out their snacks, laugh with their tablemates and select their fifteen songs to move forward in the upcoming hand tally. They avoid discussing this task, except in quiet whispers. Some can't help but lobby for their favorites, but they do so discretely.

Amber calls time and everyone returns to the tables, ready for the tally. Once Mundi volunteers call out the counts, the number of votes for each song is recorded on the large posters that were put up on the walls at the beginning of the day.

It's immediately clear that nearly one-third of the songs cannot move forward since they garnered only a few votes. Amber asks permission that those with the fewest votes be let go. Occasionally someone will raise a question or defend a piece for its uniqueness that no one else has noticed. Otherwise, the group deletes the songs with the fewest votes. Tara, Mary, and Micki, the assistants for the day, place an "x" next to those while everyone else quietly watches. Then Amber stares at the posters before asking the group, "Can we all agree that if a song received more than twenty votes it automatically advances?" She scans the head nods. "We have consensus." Volunteers asterisk the six songs with the most votes. "We have twenty songs left that need to be discussed for the twelve places remaining for this year's repertoire." This is perhaps the most draining and difficult part of the day since it requires fierce concentration as members debate the inclusion of various songs and their rationale. Soon the Mundis will vote with stickers, and only a percentage of the songs will remain in the discussion. This finely tuned process is moving along relatively efficiently, but that's not the way it started when it was a weekend retreat at the beach.

"What happens at the coast, stays at the coast." –Anonymous

Song Selection didn't always operate so seriously with so many strong protocols. The first one was held in 1991 after the second season. Karm explains, "I couldn't keep doing 'Don't Fence Me In' or whatever Sweet Honey [in the Rock] was doing." Lisa adds, "The very first Song Selection was held after a rehearsal, as the membership was less than twenty-five. A dozen women gathered around a large boombox with a box of cassette tapes that had been submitted. However, there was no formal process as they began their task. After three songs, one Mundi announced that the chorus should only sing songs written by women, for women, and about women. While she spoke, another Mundi looked through the songs being considered and told us there would only be one song to consider."

When it wasn't part of the business meeting, Song Selection was a joyous—sometimes raucous and bawdy—trip to the coast. Many recall the "yellow house," a rental that was used for the business aspect of the trip as well as a giant slumber party where there could be two or three to a bed. (Those seeking more privacy or space, and who had the financial means, would rent other places nearby, camp in vans, or camp on the beach.) People arrived on Friday night or early Saturday morning, enjoyed a group breakfast and then got together for the task at hand—choosing the music to be sung the following season. Sometimes leadership would meet on Friday afternoon for business, but Friday night was often a party. In the early years there wasn't any alcohol, but later the rule was relaxed.

Sylvia remembers, "On Saturday morning, everyone handed their tapes or CDs to the facilitator, Do Mi Stauber, and we'd spend at least an hour or two writing down the song names on our own piece of paper. Then the facilitator would play the beginning of each song until the group felt they had heard enough. That's like what we do today but the details are vastly different."

Kay adds, "And many were terribly hungover that Saturday morning. In some ways that was helpful."

In the early years, it was up to the people there to determine this process, but it always involved listening and notetaking, discussion, voting, and some type of closure for the process. Sometimes those gathered would debate the chorus's goals or mission; other times they considered what the audience would enjoy. Debates could get intense if people were attached to their submissions. Since submissions weren't anonymous, harsh criticism could be received poorly, and sometimes people had trouble letting go of a song they personally loved but the group didn't want to choose. Of course, technical difficulties occurred (*e.g.,* tape player/boombox failure, poor sound quality), further slowing the process.

It took all day to listen to the dozens of songs submitted by the Mundis. At times, hearing a selection triggered a thought from someone, who would then run out to her car and find a tape or CD with another song to add. The discussion of the songs and the paring down to a manageable list took the whole day with a break for lunch. After the work was done, the fun began—a potluck dinner together, and weather permitting, a fire on the beach with clothing optional dancing. They gathered and laughed and sang, strengthening their community in such a way that only happens through extensive interactions.

Cathy provides an easy analogy. "When we're flipping burgers at the barbeque, we're out there and you're talking to others about life. I have two boys and all of a sudden, you're learning the same about someone who doesn't sit in your section. That can't happen after rehearsal where you hear, 'I've got a pet sitter so I have to get home, or I have to run to the grocery store.' We just don't meet people [outside of our section] in the same way."

Eventually more ground rules and education were provided, as each Song Selection was a learning experience. Lisa states, "When the music committee started pre-screening to save time, we would sometimes leave a song in the mix that was too soloistic or difficult so we could educate the group."

"We have eighty members and over a hundred
opinions."—Lisa

At today's Song Selection, Mexican food awaits the hungry chorus. As they file through the line, the mood lightens and soon people are joking and laughing. Sylvia uses the time to prepare for the next task of the afternoon—voting. Each member of the chorus, including the music directors, gets a set number of dots; how many dots is determined by how many songs remain. This year the number is ten. As the members finish eating, they head to the wall of posters and place a dot next to the ten songs they would like to see advance. A few have formed alliances with friends, and they place dots on some of the same songs, while others spend time reviewing their notes thoroughly before making a single choice. The entire process takes a half hour, and once all the dots are placed, Amber and her assistants count the votes.

Amber gives the group time to study the dots on the chart. She then reminds the group, "For those of you who are new, the chorus picks roughly two-thirds of the music, and the directors choose up to one-third. Sometimes they choose to add a song we rejected, or they bring back a song from previous years, or they've found some cool new stuff for us to do. This year we're trying to select no more than nineteen songs. Also, it's important to note that even though we might choose a song, if the musical directors just cannot create a good arrangement for our chorus, they can set it aside."

Now she points to some circled songs, which have the lowest votes. "Let's see if there are some we can let go. Who wants to comment?" she asks, beginning a discussion of whether any of these songs have enough value to keep in the mix. When she gets stuck, she moves to the songs that got the most votes, attempting to "lock in" some of the favorites in each genre, and keeping care to balance the program.

"When you think about some of the crazy songs we choose, and the work Lisa does after Song Selection, arranging the songs so we can sing them... The amount of music she arranges is incredible. As a musician, I know I don't have that capability. She's extremely gifted at what she does."—Becky Bailey

Lisa remembers how she and Karm would often meet during the Song Selection weekend at the coast after the chorus had finished the process. "Over burgers at the Flounder Tavern in Waldport, we'd divide the songs. It was like, 'Oh, this one's your style,' or 'That one's right up your alley.'"

Both membership and musical directors have always faced challenges with Song Selection, as the "Soromundi Way" of valuing everyone's opinion overrides the general criteria most choruses employ to select their repertoire. There is little the directors can be sure of when the season starts. While the Mundis are given guidelines for Song Selection, many songs are pet favorites and derive from the passion of the person who suggests it. For the musical directors, arranging the songs is a challenge, especially in a non-audition chorus where the membership ranges from pitch problematic to highly trained. As the goal is to sing in four to eight parts—soprano, alto, tenor, bass with splits in each section to high/low—arranging songs without knowing who will show up in September is a leap of faith. Which section will be the largest? Will the strongest singers return? Will strong singers suddenly change sections because an ex-girlfriend is singing in last year's section? Whose voice may have changed?

For a traditional choral piece, arranging in SATB is hard enough, but adjusting range and difficulty across all the genres and styles that Soromundi sings is quite a feat. In any given performance, audiences may hear Lady Gaga's "Telephone" followed by "The 23rd Psalm."

Lisa says, "I hate to sound rude, but Karm and I started a code, KMN. It means Kill Me Now. It refers to a song that someone in chorus suggested, but neither one of wants to arrange or direct. Of course, we would never say that or let it be known, but sometimes we are completely baffled by a song. Fortunately, at this point, the choir is pretty skilled and those now fall away quickly in the process."

> "At Song Selection everyone gets a slice of the pie of equal value, regardless of what they bring."—Assistant Director Lynn Smith

Two hours have passed, and the conversation has circled back to a song that didn't make the cut. The group is fatigued but some are silent while others are joining the speaker in asking for it to move up for consideration. Amber seems uncomfortable with the request and looks to the board president and Lisa for guidance. The Soromundi Way encourages everyone to speak her/their mind, even if the opinion has changed over lunch. Eventually the song is back in the mix for consideration.

Once all of the discussion concludes, twenty-one songs remain. Lisa raises her hand and once she's acknowledged by Amber, she says, "I'd just like to remind everyone that with the choices we've made, we're very heavy on the contemporary pop tunes. Since part of our past is folk music and circle songs, just as examples, if you want any say on which of those we'll include, think about what's left to discuss."

The group spends the last half hour finalizing their list, heeding Lisa's advice and identifying two folk songs that might work. When the final song is circled by Amber, the group shouts and whoops at the list. Someone sitting near Lisa asks, "Are these good ones?" meaning, can she and Lynn arrange the choices.

Lisa laughs and replies, "We'll see."

"Song Selection is an amazing process that feels unique to our choir. I am so grateful for the work and people that came before me to make this process smooth and accessible each year. I learn something new every time that helps me be a better choir member and person."—Amber

The Song Selection weekends of the past became more difficult as the chorus grew. It wasn't feasible to house sixty people, and many couldn't make the trip. The chorus wanted to encourage participation, but a significant number couldn't afford a weekend away, in money, time, or both. Accessibility was also an issue for people with mobility challenges. The leadership realized Song Selection needed to change. Moreover, the line between the "work" of Soromundi and the behavior of some after hours, including excessive drinking, became a potential insurance liability.

As the community building piece remained essential, a potential compromise was attempted in 2012 when Song Selection happened at the beach for those who could go and remotely in Eugene at a chorus member's home. Amber served as the facilitator that year and remembers, "It created a lot of challenges since we were in two different places, and there wasn't Zoom yet. We used video/Skype via a phone system. There were many issues. People couldn't hear. The connection wasn't great. Also, the lack of togetherness brought out unusual attitudes, as people behave much differently as a small group over remote video than they do in a larger, face to face facilitated session. Some people at the remote location had very strident voices about what should be chosen, and some of the people there felt very uncomfortable."

That fact coupled with the technology issues faced by the low-tech communication proved to the leadership that Song

Selection functioned best with the entire group together. By the next year Song Selection became a one-day, local activity. Sylvia revamped much of the process, focusing the discussion on the key issues necessary to have the chorus vote for their choices and utilizing the advancements in technology.

Regardless of where the process occurs, eighty-five to ninety percent of the songs recommended by the chorus are performed by the chorus. Lisa adds, "Song Selection continues to be a place where we educate ourselves, allowing for discussion about cultural appropriation, gender diversity, and other critical themes." There are former songs—ones that were enthusiastically recommended during Song Selection and well received when first performed—that won't be sung again. A few years ago, the song, "I Lost My Talk," was removed from consideration during Song Selection as it featured "throat singing," a technique specific to, in this case, the Inuit Indigenous people. The same is true for costume choices. The flamboyant, colorful "sarongs" that made the Mundis stand out at the GALA event, have been shelved in favor of a more uniform look—black shirts, pants/skirts, socks, and shoes.

Song Selection has proven effective for over three decades. How can this be with such a wide range of songs, which will be sung by many people with no training, some of whom aren't yet in the non-audition chorus? These factors would make most musical directors cringe, yet Lisa is its staunchest defender. "This process is so unique to this group, and it also bonds us together. By the end of it, we're tired, but we inevitably find compromise. It's not even the final list I care about. Listening and watching the group tells me all the things I need to know—how committed they are to some songs, where concerns were raised about content, which lyrics moved them, who are our future chorus leaders, who is stubborn and might cause dissent. And after each Song Selection, I come away very proud to be a part of this group. Then I take a deep breath and say to myself, 'Let the fun begin!'"

Song Selection is without a doubt the heaviest lift each year, but it yields the greatest rewards, as each member has a voice in the upcoming season. What began as an informal gathering at the coast became an annual exercise of empowerment that still holds true to the feminist ideas that were the foundation of Soromundi in 1989.

TWELVE

Leadership structure has greatly changed throughout Soromundi's history. The consensus model, rooted in early feminism, evolved to a more traditional structure and introduced the "Modern Era." It should be acknowledged, though, during those early decades leaders emerged and walked a narrow tightrope, helping the organization move forward with most of the membership alongside them. Not an easy task.

In the summer of 2024, the four women who have served as presidents since the 2006 restructuring, the beginning of the "Modern Era," sat down to talk about their experiences, what they've learned, and the future of Soromundi. Co-author Ann Roberts served as moderator.

Linda Cipriano, 2006-2011
Amber Smith, 2011-2016
Kate Barry, 2016-2022
Micki Varner, 2022-June, 2025
Ann: How did each of you find Soromundi and how did you become involved with the Board of Directors?

Linda: I joined the chorus in 1995. I was oblivious to what had happened [Karm's departure]. I didn't know about all the drama. I just came because I wanted to sing. I had moved here from the Bay Area. I was in a women's chorus, not a lesbian chorus, for many years. I saw Soromundi sing at the 1994 Eugene Celebration. They were on the Broadway Mall under a tent. I think there might have been twelve of them, and I thought, "Well, that's interesting." I was just coming out as a lesbian in my late forties, so I thought that might be fun. I think Lisa approached me and asked if I wanted to be treasurer. At that point we had a business committee that maybe had changed to an "operations" committee. I was treasurer for three years, and then I was... (*looks at the group*) "co" something?

Kate: We didn't really have a president but sometimes people would proclaim themselves as president.

(Laughter)

Linda: Anyway, I don't remember. And then when we decided to go to a formal board structure, I went into the meeting with Julie Weisman thinking I wouldn't mind being president. I don't even remember how that came about.

Ann: You probably went to the bathroom.

(Laughter).

Linda: Yeah, I was okay with it because I'd had some experience with boards, and I thought I could be a good manager.

Amber: I joined chorus in 2000 when I was a sophomore at the University of Oregon. I'd seen a poster at Mother Kali's. I was hanging out with gay men, and that wasn't the best way to meet any ladies. I'm very shy, though, and so when I showed up to rehearsal by myself, I was greeted by Amber Dennis, who was giving hugs. I thought to myself, "Are we dating now?" *(Laughter)* Not really, but you know what I mean? I like to make people comfortable, so I gravitated toward the social committee. At the time we were doing greeting cards for people and social graces now known as "checking in" with people]. Then I became membership chair and then president. I'd had very little experience on a board, so there was a lot of handholding. Pat Vallerand helped me immensely, and one person suggested I do some reading to be a better president. *(Laughter)* Lisa also kept reminding me to make it my own and own whatever happened.

I should also mention I wasn't a singer, and had it not been a non-audition chorus, and if I hadn't seen Soromundi perform, I wouldn't have joined. So, I just walked in blindly, hoping to be a part of a community that was going to be friendly, gentle, and queer.

Kate: I joined in 1994, and I joined because I loved singing when I was younger. I'm a feminist and Soromundi was a lesbian chorus. It was a very interesting experience because Karm had left the year before and Lisa had become the director. There were still a lot of undercurrents and tension, and it felt very much like an "us against them," and which side are you on? Half of the people didn't speak to me. Luckily, I was in the altos and Marty and Pamela did speak to me. Fortunately, I really wanted to sing. Otherwise, I don't think I would've continued.

I got involved with the organization because Lisa and I had a meeting in my living room with the people on the de facto business committee, trying to figure out where the chorus should move because of the tension. Is the focus music? Is it politics? Being a proper lesbian? Then I became a section leader. After that, I backed off for a while because of my job, but then, Linda, in the last year of her presidency, asked if I would co-chair the Northwest Tour. Eventually, I became the concerts chair and then president for six years. I'd wanted to do five, but then Covid happened, and each board member decided to stay on for an extra year.

Micki: I joined the chorus in the fall of 2011. I'd seen the chorus perform a few times, and I thought that when life got less crazy, I'd join. So I joined in 2011 and tried to keep my leadership skills on the downlow because I joined chorus to have fun in my life. *(Laughter)* I guess I didn't hide it very well. I was recruited for the board in 2015 after being section leader. I did a lot with rehearsals and retreats, and then Kate approached me about becoming vice president and her successor. I stayed an extra year as vice president during Covid, and then I became president in 2022.

What were some of the key issues during your presidency, the biggest challenges you faced?

Linda: I think my greatest challenge was being first with the new board structure. We were just trying to find our footing, and I used any kind of management skills and leadership skills I had. One issue that came up around 2010 was a situation about women-only events. The organizer of a particular event declared it to be for women only. It didn't come to the board. She just declared it.

Ann: How did you deal with that?

Linda: Well, we created an online forum so that people could speak their piece. We created a policy that said we'd have women-only events, we'd have events with little kids, and we'd have other social events where men could be present. I don't think we ever had all of those because that's a lot of events.

Micki: Fast forward to last year when people thought we still had that policy in place, and many of us had never heard of it.

Linda: Yeah.

Ann: One of the things Kate and I realized during our research is that fifteen years passed between Soromundi becoming a non-profit organization and this new structure. Do you remember having any pushback about the new structure, one that had really been eschewed by previous leadership for being too patriarchal?

Linda: I did not. I think the membership had changed enough. The personalities of the group were more open to this structure.

Kate: There weren't as many personal agendas.

Amber: I think part of the challenge with an all-volunteer board is that we don't always have the same person collecting all these things. And then we're trying to find stuff, but some of it hasn't been documented. The volunteers change over time, and you don't necessarily remember the resolution, but you just remember that there was a high adrenaline fight over it. I remember in my time, there was conversation about kids. How old can kids be to attend a rehearsal or event? Sometimes our comfort level changes, and we can't remember the decision.

Linda: One other thing I remember was how we defined a Soromundi activity. There was an event being planned and the organizer didn't invite all of Soromundi, but she called it a Soromundi activity. We determined that if you call it a Soromundi event, then everyone gets invited.

Ann: Amber, you mentioned the kid discussion, but what else was a challenge?

Amber: We were getting pretty big and kind of unwieldy, and as a non-audition chorus, sometimes people came and went. We were trying to be accessible, but there were some folks who were there for the singing and some were there just for the community. When I came on as president, I didn't want to make big changes immediately. So, the issue of Song Selection [where it should be held] was a hot topic, and also we were trying to figure out what it means to be a board member. I had to talk to people about whether they were a good fit for the board.

Also, we were having conversations about being a non-audition chorus, being accessible to all, but when you get larger, what does that look like? We tried having two choruses, where one was geared toward people who had sung for a long time, maybe could read music. And the other chorus just showed up, didn't want to talk about the politics. I think we're still struggling with that, where we're working on talking about gender and inclusivity. We had a lot of big needs people during my years, and I was at the forefront, so I had to communicate with those people. We had a Song Selection where some people were feeling very unsafe, and that was the first time we had Song Selection in two places.

Ann: I wasn't around then, so I'm not sure what you're

talking about.

Amber: We had the same Song Selection but one was remote.

Linda: We didn't have Zoom, so it was just a call-in thing.

Amber: And at some point, one person got very upset about a song and very adamant about why we should or shouldn't choose it, and the people in the remote location didn't feel comfortable at all. So, yeah, I think this all stemmed from managing a large chorus.

Ann: Kate, what about you? What was your biggest challenge?

Kate: The biggest issue was Covid, but I'll talk about that last. I don't know if it was because we [much of the membership] had reached a certain age, but a lot of people passed during my tenure. At one point I thought, "I hope I never have to send this communication out again." There was Pat, then Breeze, then Cindy, Victoria, Susan, and our darling Lynne. I felt like I was sending out a death notice every week. And [as the president] trying to find the balance between holding everyone's emotions and acknowledging them, while helping us stay together as a chorus...and moving forward. What was the appropriate ceremony and recognition? During all of it, Lisa and I talked continually, which helped.

And another thing was that we had to dismiss somebody from chorus. That was only the second time that had ever occurred. We realized early on with this issue that we needed a harassment policy as well as a grievance policy. In the end, it took us two years from the initial complaint to the dismissal. There were steps like having a mentor, talking with me. I'd call Pat [an attorney and a Mundi] asking her if something was legal.

When a second person came forward with a complaint, I told Lisa we had to do something. So, in the end we did get a clear process for grievances and a clear structure for making those decisions.

The major challenge was Covid. We were preparing for our 30th Anniversary Tour in California, and we had a Reunion Chorus planned, and a recording. We had done one concert at the Shedd with the Eugene Gay Men's Chorus at the end of February 2020... And then it all went away. We had a year (the 20/21 season) completely on Zoom, then tried to resume rehearsals the following season. We were in and out of different places, masked, socially distant, trying to remain a functioning chorus while responding to everyone's fears. Eventually we had a few short weeks before the spring concert. And Lisa, bless her heart, thought we could do a concert *and* make a recording. And she was right. She led us through all of it.

Ann: It almost sounds like you were on 24/7.

Kate: I was retired, fortunately. I'd never have been able to do it and have a job.

Ann: I imagine a lot of them just needed support.

Kate: Yes, people called all the time just needing to talk. People needed a lot of personal love.

Micki: While you were talking about coming back together, Kate, it felt as though every time we would send out an announcement about moving forward, there would be ten well-researched emails in reply about why we should not, including links to articles, and stats, and graphs.

Kate: It was a lot of anxiety, which is perfectly understandable. We were anxious too.

Amber: That's why I took myself out. I was like, I just can't.

Ann: Okay, Micki, what was your biggest challenge?

Micki: So, in 21-22, we had only come back from the pandemic partially. We had the "Covid Chorus." It was all returning members, but it was smaller [since many veteran members hadn't come back yet], and we did one performance and made the recording. The next year, 22-23, when we came back fully in person, taking new members, a full calendar of events, and the release of that recording... It was like waking up from a long sleep of two and a half years.

So, bringing it all back online, it felt like we had to remember, "How did we do that thing?" Like with T-shirt orders. It was like, "Oh, crap. We've got new members, so we've got to order shirts." Small details to big things. Then, a huge issue emerged about men at rehearsal. There were also communication issues within the leadership, but at least we were all reasonably in tune. But we were still coming out of the pandemic where our sense of personal space was redefined. Finding space where eighty to a hundred people can comfortably rehearse, have resources like a decent piano, good sight lines, plenty of chairs... It was very challenging and is still challenging.

And of course, that was on top of our usual challenges—social media, website maintenance, and being an all-volunteer organization that tries to meet all of its operational needs. It's based on chance that we're going to have the skill sets we need in the chorus, or how do we provide for what's missing? Sometimes the professions of our members line up nicely with what we need, and sometimes they don't. So, sustaining the all-volunteer organization is a big challenge.

Our next question is the question that drove Kate and I to do this whole project. As our leaders, why do you believe Soromundi has lasted for thirty-five years and how do we move forward into the future?

Linda: I've said this a million times. We've lasted because we've been willing to adapt to the times and the changing culture yet maintaining faithfulness to our history and purpose.

Kate: Amen.

Linda: Another reason is because our singing repertoire is unlike any other chorus. We're different and I hope we remain that way to sustain.

Amber: For me, it's about singing together. We all come with our own stories, and we bring those stories to the table, but they're not the focus. It's about being part of the community. It's not about a specific person because we have turnover and we don't implode, right? We're all coming together with the idea that the singing is primary. And I think Song Selection is a huge piece because we have an investment in what we're singing.

I do think we need to figure out how to get more people into the chorus, because we'll continue to lose people because of aging, relationships, whatever. I just want to make sure it's a welcoming place.

Kate: I would say that, first and foremost, Lisa is the key figure in the chorus's history. When Karm left, if Lisa had not stepped forward, the chorus would not be. We would've been the same as every other organization who had dissipated over conflict. And I also think the chorus's capacity to change has been a part of it. I'm thinking about the structure, when Julie [Weisman] came in and said you need a real board. Well, let's have a board. Let's do this properly. And something Julie said when Ann and I interviewed her... She said, "Do you know you are my example of the most sustainable non-profit in the state in terms of your membership and the fact that you are led entirely by volunteers."

And it's not just board members. It's a lot of volunteers. People willing to step up and give time. Soromundi is more than a chorus. It's a community. For some, Soromundi is like a church.

Amber: That's how I think of it.

Kate: It's about community and relationships. It's a huge part of why we've sustained. People love us because of what we've given. So for us to continue, we'll have to change and grow. We have to remember our mission, which is both about making music and reaching out.

Micki: I think the stability of Lisa's leadership has to be called out—everything she brings musically, relationally, and the charisma of her personality. Her continuous association with the leadership of the chorus. Also, I think even with all the personality challenges, we seem to have attracted people who bring an understanding of leadership, service and a willingness to volunteer. You have to be ready to work. We know there are some unsung heroes along the way who've been informal leaders, who've done the same tasks over and over for twenty-plus years, and they form a bedrock.

When I think about the future, I think about the under-forty members moving into informal and formal leadership roles. I think we'll have to get a vision for who we can be without Lisa when she decides to retire. I got into it once with someone who said, "Well, when Lisa decides she doesn't want to do chorus anymore, then the chorus won't exist." And I lost it. Why have we done so much work to develop policies, become a 501c(3), develop structures and roles, if we aren't going to move into the future? And I think about what we can do to sustain a culture of service and volunteerism. Because if we don't, we're going to have to radically increase our budget and hire staff. And I don't think we want to be that group.

Last question: How do you define The Soromundi Way?

Linda: THE SOROMUNDI WAY:
1. No one is turned away due to lack of funds, be it dues or choir events, and no one is turned away for membership for any reason as long as one meets the guidelines set out by the choir.
2. The majority of our musical repertoire is selected by the membership.
3. Every aspect of keeping Soromundi running is based on volunteers.
4. If a member is uncomfortable with or opposed to any song we sing for any reason, they are free to step away during the performance of that song.
5. The "best" voice doesn't always get the solo.

Amber: The Soromundi Way involves trusting the process and bringing us together as a team to move forward. It's not focusing on the individual but on the group and how we help each other, support each other, and learn together to achieve a great performance.

Kate: The Soromundi Way allows every chorus member to have access to music regardless of background or musical education. So no auditions, help through sectionals, honoring different ways of learning. Everyone has access to the chorus regardless of their ability to pay the dues. Every chorus member has the opportunity to select the repertoire through Song Selection. Chorus members are supported in trying new things, from solos to finding their voice. Differing perspectives are honored and respected, from kneeling when singing the "National Anthem" to stepping out if lyrics are not something chorus members feel able to sing. The Soromundi Way honors music as an expression of joy and community for all.

Micki: I think it means a couple of things to me. One is "trust the process," especially in the way Lisa introduces the music, prepares us for performances, and levels up the production aspect as the season goes on. In that way, I think it's about how we navigate and weather feelings of uncertainty. Another example of this would be that moment in Song Selection when it feels like we're not making progress, but we keep talking and getting as many voices into the process as possible until the way forward emerges.

The Soromundi Way also means bringing as many members along in everything we do as much as possible. It can also be listening to that one voice that has the courage to call us back to being true to our mission. It's an expression of who we are as a community.

Ann: Thank you all for sharing your thoughts and memories today.

Thirteen

On February 15, 2020, Soromundi gave its annual Winter Concert, a collaboration with the Eugene Gay Men's Chorus (EGMC). EGMC had set a goal to collaborate with Soromundi during their first five years of existence. Soromundi wanted to offer EGMC immediate support and suggested a collaboration for their second season. It was an incredible evening and the perfect beginning to an exciting spring that included a tour, the spring concert at the Hult, and a new recording, all to celebrate Soromundi's thirtieth anniversary.

The tour committee had worked steadily since 2018 under the leadership of Rita Monasterio and Moke Varner. Several members of the Northwest Tour Committee had joined for continuity in planning, plus some new faces. The 2020 Envision Tour was scheduled for late March, a five-day itinerary with performances in Ashland, Oregon, Oakland, California, and Ukiah, California. The chorus also planned to work with various groups at each stop. The Ashland stop was sponsored by Rogue Valley Unitarian Universalist Fellowship (RVUUF), and their Social Justice Committee secured their spacious

Fellowship Hall for the concert. In Oakland the chorus planned a combined concert with two different groups: Voices: Lesbian A Cappella for Justice, and the Lesbian/Gay Chorus of San Francisco (LGCSF), at the First Unitarian Church of Oakland. In Ukiah, Soromundi planned to join the Mendocino Women's Choir for a daylong retreat and concert, with the possibility of singing with Holly Near since her sister owned the performance location—The Near & Arnold School of Performing Arts & Cultural Education (SPACE). The tour committee had reserved the Sandman motel in Santa Rosa as the Northern California base and rented two buses. One day was lightly scheduled with a plan to catch the ferry for "free time" in the city. The only singing that day was a one-hour slot that was arranged for the chorus to sing in Grace Cathedral. It wasn't a performance but more of an "opportunity of a lifetime," according to Lisa, who had performed their twice before and loved the acoustics. The arrangements were made, the deposits paid, and the itinerary confirmed. Even the music seemed to be coming together.

Although the news of a possible respiratory virus outbreak in China was reported in late 2019, in the US there were few guidelines in the early part of 2020. No one gave it much thought. Fifteen Americans had died by the night of the Winter Concert, but the Shedd Institute was packed, an indication that people weren't overly concerned. Most likely this virus would be contained soon, as most public outbreaks always had been before. No one knew that just one month later, Oregon would announce its first death from Covid-19.

Several Mundis had big plans in the coming weeks. One was celebrating a sixty-fifth birthday, and several diehard fans of the U of O Women's Basketball Team knew Sabrina Ionescu would lead the Ducks to an NCAA championship. A group of Mundis went to the regional Pac-12 championships in Las Vegas and watched the victorious Ducks cut down the net in front of huge, unmasked crowds. Yet when the Mundis returned to Eugene, the world was already changing.

"We stopped at Market of Choice on the way home," Kate states, "and people were filling their shopping carts with toilet paper and water. Shelves were emptying. We'd lived in a bubble with the tournament and had not heard much."

Soromundi leaders responded to these new developments with what they believed at the time were cautious and appropriate steps. "We were in the final preparations for the tour," Lisa remembers, "so we met to rehearse the first Tuesday in March. Many Mundis took extra precautions—no hugging, but instead elbow bumping, and they spaced themselves out."

For a short while everyone thought that chorus activities could continue with precautions. Then as facts about the virus and its transmission became known, news spread about a Washington chorus whose members had contracted Covid after a similar rehearsal, two of whom had died. California was one of first states to prohibit large gatherings and one by one, Soromundi's partnering choruses for the tour reluctantly dropped out, abiding by newly-established mandates. Lockdowns were put in place to save lives, and the tour was abandoned for the time being. Both the hotel and bus company generously agreed to roll over the deposits since the tour committee optimistically assumed the outbreak would be contained by the following year. Still, everyone was disappointed. Soromundi paused in-person rehearsals, and expectations shifted as weeks became months, and the leadership had to continually adjust to the new reality.

Unfortunately, many Mundis fell ill, but since there was no testing available yet, it was unclear if people were sick with Covid, and it was unknown where or how they had been infected. Some were concerned it may have been from the last rehearsal or an all-denominational event that had been held that week.

The board continued to meet via Zoom and collaborated with Lisa to outline a vision for the Soromundi community to stay connected for the rest of the 2019-2020 season. The tour committee grappled with unraveling the details of the tour, such as refunding deposits to those who needed the money since many suddenly experienced losing part or all their paychecks. Some Mundis were willing to let their deposits roll over, confident that the tour would happen—in 2021.

Yet, as 2020 progressed, with no vaccine or cure in sight, the board started to discuss canceling the tour entirely since only "essential" employees went to work and all indoor leisure activities remained shuttered. Like everyone, life in lockdown meant loss of work, food insecurity, caring for family, parenting and schooling children, and living in fear. Parallel goals emerged—keep Soromundi singing and keep the Soromundi community as safe and as cohesive as possible. For many Mundis, rehearsal was integral to their week, and for some, Tuesday nights were a cherished connection to the queer community. Lisa and Kate, the current Soromundi president, were besieged with emails and calls from concerned Mundis throughout the pandemic.

Welcome to the joys of Zoom! Throughout the 2020-21 season, the chorus met and rehearsed via Zoom, a great way to stay connected, but for many, a terrible way to learn music. Lisa began each Zoom rehearsal with a poll to assess the chorus's physical and mental wellness. After a virtual check-in, the rehearsal would continue with the chorus muting their sound while the directors played songs and parts. Lisa had decided to carry over some of the thirtieth-year repertoire into the 20-21 season until it was clear that the group needed to sing different material, so she added some easier songs. Zoom rehearsals were set in advance, sometimes devoted to vocal exercises, sometimes to virtual sectionals, sometimes to social sharing. Some rehearsals featured a small group at Lisa's house so members could hear the harmonies together. Various members were very innovative in nurturing social connections during this isolating time. A book club was started, discussion groups were formed to support the Black Lives Matter (BLM) movement, virtual game nights were held, and the Soromundi "campfire," allowed veterans to tell stories to the newer members. One time, Lisa prepared a scavenger hunt, requiring Mundis to run around their respective homes and gather items. When it came time to produce the items and hold them up as proof, the entire Zoom rehearsal devolved into peals of laughter.

For many Mundis, these activities were lifelines or at least momentary respites from the grief, fear, and panic that gripped each person. Some Mundis stepped away entirely, caught in the deep depression that comes with facing the death of family and friends and the loss of community. This included processing a collective grief over the passing of a dear chorus member, Lynne Graham. While Soromundi has lost many members to illness, accident, and suicide, Lynne's death was exacerbated by the fact that the Soromundi community couldn't gather to celebrate her life, support her wife, Linda, or meet, hug—and sing.

The longer the pandemic raged, the harder it was to hold the chorus and the community together. Eventually conflicts arose between Lisa and the board. Lisa had devised a structure she called singing bubbles, which would allow Mundis who were already in close proximity or social groups with each other—spouses, good friends, and family—to sing with those people. She based it on research coming out of Europe that required folks to openly discuss their exposure levels, needs, and health status. Lisa was sure that the chorus would be able to follow the guidelines she was developing.

The board was somewhat skeptical and worried that gathering the Mundis in any formation was too much of a risk.

There was still no vaccine, the US president was denying there was a pandemic, and the worst-case scenario had already happened in Seattle. The board was very focused on safety and liability. Lisa, of course, had chorus members' safety as a priority too, but thought she had a strategy to ameliorate the concerns. She also researched computer software options for singing together, and even alternative venues, such as the huge Kidspace facility, where everyone would be able to be socially distanced. However, there was still not enough known to entirely mitigate risk, especially for the population over sixty-five.

The tension was amplified by the general fear and anxiety felt by everyone as guidance on the federal level constantly changed, messaging often seemed politically motivated, and isolation continued. Kate remembers, "At one point, Lisa called me, very distressed. She felt the board was overstepping and subverting her role as music director. She likened it to the early chorus conflict with Karm, and she wondered if she should step away. As I had done in the past when other issues came up, I suggested she come to the next board meeting, and we'd all talk it out."

Lisa remembers, "I could always call Kate and say things weren't going well, or I'm not okay with something. Then she'd bring the group together and we'd deal with it. With this issue, I felt the board was taking their job very seriously to safeguard the community, but they seemed so fearful that they weren't hearing how seriously I also take my role in safeguarding our community."

The conversation proved very productive, trust was restored, and the conflicts resolved once everyone could talk in person. Lisa remembers, "I finally felt that they were hearing me and trying to understand my point of view. Not only did we need to keep physical safety in mind, but some folks had very low exposure and really *needed* to start meeting for their mental health. In turn, I really listened to the factors that the board was focused on, such as infection rates by zip codes. I think we all looked at local rates of transmission daily, and we watched the Lane County health updates each week."

Of course, there was also a feeling of missing out. Although some Mundis weren't ready to meet, they also didn't want to miss out on whatever the chorus was doing. It was truly a highly emotional time between "Soromundi the chorus" and "Soromundi the community." The board navigated the very nervous community while Lisa explored ways to bring together those who wanted to sing.

Despite the year of "no contact," there were achievements. The chorus received a grant from the Lane County Cultural Coalition to complete a marketing video in fall 2020, which is available on the website. Thanks to the efforts of resident techies, Lynn and Sylvia, in March 2021, Soromundi resumed the annual Tiny Talent Show, albeit virtually. Some acts performed live via Zoom while others submitted videos to be played. Lisa and her partner, Kiva, wrote a commemorative song, "Covid Blows," that referenced TP shortages, pee rags, fake senior IDs [to get in early to places like Costco], and green dispensaries, among other things. For many Mundis, it was a turning point toward normalcy, connecting the community, and reigniting the love of performing.

On May 19, 2021, Kate moderated a thirty-year retrospective via Zoom for the chorus and the larger community. The retrospective included the new marketing video, a panel discussion with Karm, Lisa, and Mundis Diana and Anna, an In Memoriam segment honoring the Mundis who had passed, and a slideshow of photos over the years. The program closed with a Q&A from the remote audience. This feat was only possible because of the hard work and technical skills of Mundis Lynn, Jenee, Mary, and Lori.

In the fall of 2021, Lisa and the board agreed that the

chorus could start meeting again in person—with proof of vaccination. A system was created to protect medical privacy that also ensured accountability. The board and Lisa agreed that the chorus would remain closed to new members. A hurdle occurred when it was learned the previous rehearsal space—and many other rehearsal spaces—were not open for public rental, especially to singing groups. Singing remained one of the easiest ways to transmit the virus. Lisa states, "We wanted Soromundi to be a super spreader of love, not the virus."

While a new rehearsal venue was sought, it was warm enough to be outside, so the "Masked Mundis" began the fall by gathering weekly at Wayne Morse Ranch in South Eugene. The chorus bought "singing masks," which had a peaked space in front, causing everyone to look like black-billed ducks. The large outdoor space allowed everyone to remain socially distant. Also, the idea of being back in the Soromundi community, in a setting that was regarded as highly safe by the Center of Disease Control (CDC) attracted enough of the chorus to begin rehearsing. Each week more Mundis felt safe enough to join. There was waving, talking loudly from a safe distance, and general happiness at being together again. Lisa comments, "We learned to read the smiles, even with our masks on."

Yet, as the weather grew colder, and singing outside became more difficult, the hunt for an indoor space remained elusive. Kim, the board member in charge of coordinating rehearsals and retreats, approached many different venues, emphasizing that everyone participating was vaccinated, and that masks would always be worn indoors. After much search-ing, Temple Beth Israel graciously agreed to host the chorus. Their building was closed, but they allowed the chorus access on Tuesday nights, via a custodian guarding the door. At this point, some Mundis who'd been comfortable singing outside, stepped away, especially those who had health conditions or children who couldn't be vaccinated. They felt singing inside was still too risky.

This was a time of constant adjustment. Kate remembers, "I thought of it as Command Central. It seemed that conditions and meeting guidelines were still shifting, and Lisa and I were on the phone weekly so we could adapt. At the same time, chorus members were understandably anxious, and we needed to respond to their concerns and be attentive to the guidelines set out specifically for singers. We did our best to handle every situation and answer every question."

Just as the chorus was adapting to rehearsal at Temple Beth Israel, another variant emerged, and rehearsing was once again halted. After a few weeks, the leadership agreed that in-person rehearsing could recommence, and a new location was sought. While the chorus was grateful to Temple Beth Israel, it had not been the ideal place, and paying for the custodian had been expensive. Some venues were starting to reopen and the chorus returned to a place they knew well, First United Methodist Church, affectionately known as "The Toaster Church" because of its design. The church allowed Soromundi to rehearse in its enormous sanctuary; however, the number of people who could gather was restricted. Lisa and Assistant Director Lynn split the chorus in two groups— altos and sopranos rehearsed the first hour, and tenors and basses the second. Between the rehearsals would be thirty minutes of "HVAC time," allowing the air to clear before the next group entered. The game of musical rehearsal places would continue twice more until Soromundi finally settled into a place and returned to weekly rehearsals. However, even as the choir returned to in-person rehearsals, because of masking, no one could hear instructions about what they were supposed to be doing. It was still enormously difficult for the chorus to make strong progress, though the community was starting to regain confidence about health and safety.

It was obvious by January that there wouldn't be any tour in the near future, so the board handled all the financial pieces and archived all the notes, emails, and logistics for another year. Soromundi had tentatively booked the Hult Center for their spring concert in May 2022, hopeful that their standing engagement in the Soreng could still happen, but it was unclear when concert venues would reopen. There were only about sixty singers and only a few weeks of rehearsals to practice in sections without masks before the concert. Kate recalls, "One night at rehearsal, Lisa announced that she was not only confident we could pull off a concert, which many of us were not, but that she planned for us to complete the long-awaited recording. Everyone took a lot of deep breaths, but once we recovered, we realized if Lisa believed we could do it, we would try."

And they did. Affectionately known as The Covid Chorus, the smaller chorus performed that concert, supported by a short set from the Motet Singers, a local acapella vocal ensemble. A few weeks later, Soromundi returned to the Shedd Institute to make the recording that had been planned two years prior. The place where they'd last performed, just before the pandemic closed the doors on all their plans, was now the location of their new beginning. Lisa states, "It may not be our best recording, but it will always be the one that means the most to me. Every voice on that CD worked so hard, conquered their fears, handled their personal situations, and, yes, basked in enough good luck that let them be present."

When September of 2022 arrived, Soromundi returned to a normal season. Kate finally stepped down as president, and Micki became the new president. New members were once again invited to join, and the new leadership, had to "re-

remember" all the protocols and systems the chorus usually followed during a "normal" year, reaching back to a time that seemed so long ago. Zoom became a tool that allowed ill or absent members to watch a rehearsal from home, continuing the vigilance regarding the health and welfare of the Soromundi community. The recordings could also be reviewed by all of the chorus members trying to learn a difficult part of the repertoire.

The recording made at the Shedd "dropped" in early January of 2023, and a release party was scheduled. It was the first indoor social event the choir held in over two years with food, drinks, dancing, decorations, a DJ, and photo area, all made possible by a generous donor. It was a recognition of what had been accomplished, what *most* had survived, and a celebration because it was, as the recording's title track said, "Good to be Alive."

FOURTEEN

I t's only 6:15 p.m. on a Tuesday evening in early May 2025. Soromundi's spring performance in the Soreng is just a few weeks away. The sun is sticking around longer these days, so many of the Mundis wait in their cars with the windows down, enjoying the spring air, talking on their phones or eating their dinner. Another group mills on the sidewalk, chatting and laughing. President Micki Varner and her wife, Moke, pull into a parking spot. At the sight of the person with the key, several Mundis leave their vehicles and join the group.

As everyone starts inside, Tara, the membership chair, approaches, her arms full of supplies. Two Mundis rush to help her. Tonight, the Reunion Chorus (RC), a mix of Mundis from various years and decades, will join the chorus for rehearsal and sing several songs in each half of the spring concert. Tara's job is to make sure each RC member signs in, has a nametag, and knows where to go.

Everyone else heads for the storage closet as the carts full of chairs are wheeled out. The setup crew is larger tonight and includes section leaders and members of the DEIB team. They volunteered to come early to assist the RC members and make sure they have their music and remember where to sit. Thirty extra chairs must be arranged, making the total 120 seats. Fortunately, the rehearsal space, a fellowship hall of an Episcopalian church, is cavernous and can handle the seating arrangement. Two Mundis push the grand piano across the room, a generous donation from earlier this year.

Mundi Shawn and other helpers conference quickly and start building the rows. Someone calls out, "How are we doing this?"

"We're in sections," Shawn replies. Each section will sit together to ensure the Reunion Chorus has support as they learn their parts.

Tara has her table ready and is taking attendance as the RC members tend to arrive early. Against the bank of windows, Moke, the cashier, and Rebecca, the treasurer, have set up their table, and Moke's cashbox is at the ready to take donations, dues, and tonight, most likely money for the baseball jerseys some Mundis have purchased. Often there are financial questions, so it is helpful if the treasurer is always in the same place each week, especially with a chorus of ninety.

As the clock approaches 6:35 p.m., more Mundis have wandered in. They welcome the Reunion Chorus members with smiles and hugs all round. It's fun to see people again, sometimes after years of absence. All section leaders are present and taking attendance. Kamela, soprano section leader, notices there is a chair missing from the front row, and she heads back to the closet to retrieve one.

"Don't forget to give me your jersey money!" Moke calls out, and a few Mundis break away from their conversations and head toward her table.

A crowd is forming around the back counter. Mundi Lori has brought a card for people to sign and a brown envelope to collect donations for the previous rehearsal space, a church that was severely vandalized the weekend before. A few veteran Mundis are recounting the kindness and support of the pastor to newer members. All are shocked. Sadness and anger color the conversation of those who sign the card and hand over some cash.

Assistant Director Lynn arrives and heads for the piano. She arranges some of the music for the night, and Anne, alto section leader, approaches, asking her to play a few measures, a part the altos can't seem to get right. Rehearsal is one of Lynn's happy places. "What we build together in rehearsal...the act of being together...it's more important than the final product. We're a community, a sisterhood."

At 6:45 p.m., Lisa and her wife Kiva arrive. Five Mundis start in her direction but don't invade her personal space until she's settled at the piano. They can't help but look like they're ready to pounce. Lisa makes eye contact with the Mundi closest to her and the others seem to form a line.

Shoshi is setting up the laptop for the evening's "Zoomers." One of the few silver linings of the pandemic was establishing a way for ill, injured, and tonight, out-of-town Reunion Chorus members, to experience rehearsal. She asks Lisa, "Will you start rehearsal at the piano or the podium?"

Lisa replies, "Piano."

Another Mundi, also named Lori, holds a clipboard and is darting from group to group, asking if anyone can chaperone Eugene's Pink Prom, the prom held specifically for queer students. Apparently there has been concern about haters harassing the attendees as they enter The Lavender Network, the new queer center.

Dawn, the Marketing Director, lays out posters to be distributed throughout the community by Mundis. Curious people huddle around the table, nodding and smiling at the original artwork.

It's now 6:53 p.m. Rose Mary, the "master hugger" of

Soromundi, draws a smile from each person she greets, making everyone feel special and seen. Mary, the techie, has set up the microphone for Lisa. In the new space, especially with 120 people, it's necessary, even though Lisa has a teacher voice that projects. Bert, another techie, checks in with Lisa about the sound needs for the dress rehearsals on May 13th and May 15th.

The four Mundi string players gather and prepare to go practice in another part of the building. Becky, who was at one point the youngest Mundi, chats with Alanna, the youngest Mundi currently. When asked how Soromundi can last for another thirty-five years, Alanna replies, "We just need to keep reaching out to the young people." A look around the room at the amount of younger people indicates Soromundi is trending in the right direction.

A survey conducted a few years ago indicated that only fifty-two percent of the Mundis at that time identified as lesbian. While Alanna doesn't identify as a lesbian, she doesn't have a problem with the chorus's name. "I understand that I stand on the shoulders of women who risked so much just to be who they are and be called lesbian. I'm fine with it." While Alanna is the youngest, there are many first- and second-year members who are Millennials. Some of them may leave because they are students, have other interests, or find it just isn't the best fit, but Soromundi's non-audition status will continue to symbolize an open door and an opportunity for them to return in the future, as so many Mundis have in the past.

No auditions. A rule most choir directors couldn't fathom or condone for long. Yet, Lisa and Karm relish it. Becky explains, "The non-audition piece is the heart of Soromundi. Without it, the spirit of Soromundi would be lost. We are sisters of the world. It's not about who can sing the best, who's the prettiest, who has the largest bank account. It's *all* of us together."

Karm arrives carrying the Ugandan drum she will play on "Adiemus." This year she has emerged from retirement, no longer arranging and teaching, but having the honor (according to her), of directing some numbers, playing on some others, and singing bass. Every time she enters a room, steps behind the podium, or finishes directing a song, a few—and sometimes many—start applauding or calling her name. They want her to know how appreciated she is for what she started. And who knows? Perhaps she'll stay another year.

It's 7:00 p.m. Lisa starts playing "Proud Mary," an understood signal for the chorus to take their seats. Everyone peels away from their conversations after finishing one more sentence. Many join the song's chorus, "Rolling...rolling... rolling on the river." They bop to their seats, sing it like Tina Turner, or ham it up. It takes another thirty seconds for the Soromundi community to transform into Soromundi Lesbian Chorus of Eugene.

Suddenly Lisa stops playing, looks up and smiles. "Okay, let's get started."

KARM'S TOP 10 SONGS

We asked Karm to name and explain her Top 10 songs Soromundi has performed.

1. Love, Rescue Me - Sheryl's pure voice, the message, the energy our choir brought, and that I found it from a Protestant and Catholic mixed youth choir in Northern Ireland.

2. Rainbow Connection – This song gives me hope more than any other and I will always get choked up at the stanza, "Who said that every wish would be heard and answered, when wished on the morning star? Somebody thought of that, and someone believed it. Look what it's done so far." Someday we'll find it...! I'm sad that it never made it on to a CD.

3. Durmé – A shephardic folk song, Audrey Snyder's haunting arrangement, how the piece soars with that tenor line at the perfect place, the beauty of the language.

4. Invocation – A May Sarton poem perfectly set to music - the minor key at the beginning, the rhythm that suggests the tides rolling in and out, where it peaks at "love touch us everywhere" and comes back down with "with primeval candor." And I'm going to love any song that contains the word "architrave."

5. Song of Peace, Finlandia - The message is that there is beauty all over the world. The chord progression to "my hopes, my dreams, my holy shrine." A true song of peace.

6. Choose Something Like a Star – Love this for so many reasons. I sang it in high school in 1966 and loved it then. It was only six years old at the time! I love the poem; I love the music. A favorite of all time. To get to direct it for the 35th Anniversary is such an honor.

7. Tumbling Tumbleweeds - I sang it in the car as a little kid riding along with my folks and it was one of many songs where I learned how to harmonize. So in Year One I used it to teach people what harmony is and how to be confident holding a part that might not be the melody.

8. Seasons of Love - I love the litany of all the things contained in 525,600 minutes. So human. How do you measure a year? In love, of course. Measure in love.

9. Circle of Life - This was my favorite solo as well as another chance to get down with Mundi Amy Picard! The choir really brought it, too, so it was fun to just let it loose and be supported.

10. You Are the New Day - More about hope and love wrapped in a beautiful melody to pass along to the

next ones. How can we not move forward upon hearing:

"One more day when time is running out
For everyone
Like a breath I knew would come I reach for
The new day
Hope is my philosophy
Just needs days in which to be
Love of life means hope for me
Borne on a new day
You are the new day!

LISA'S TOP 10 SONGS

1. Harriet Tubman – One of the earliest songs I learned with Soromundi. I was classically trained and had no idea how to play by ear or make an accompaniment. I loved the social justice messages, the history, and the arrangement.

2. Something Inside So Strong – Don't misunderstand; I NEVER want to perform this song ever again (since we've sung it several times). However, there was never a better "message" song. It was an "in your face" reminder that being LGBTQ+ is not a choice, is not bad, and is not to be justified... But to be a lesbian is coveted and we are proud of who we are. Audiences had never heard that, and many of us had never been given permission to feel that way.

3. Circle is Cast – So many of us were backing out of *all* the mainstream social constructs we were taught as children, and one of those was organized religion. We were open and eclectic, exploring all type of spiritual journeys while we were waiting

for Christian churches to come around. Some were so traumatized that they couldn't set foot in a church. This song gave voice, not only to the beliefs in the power of our own strength, but it celebrated the elements of Mother Earth. It even gave us a chance to learn about the history of casting out the "witches" and healers who had different beliefs. I love the way we would chant the goddesses at the end from across the room, and I can't imagine the song without Linda Lou's amazing solo.

4. Beating Heart – Looking back, this was super hard for us at the time—the first time I arranged tone clusters for the group. The piece is rhythmic—or even hypnotic, but there were lots of technical things we were learning to do! *And* Marty added amazing drums.

5. Circle Me, Sisters – Love the message *and* it's the first arrangement I composed that I didn't hate. I might even say I'm a little proud of that one.

6. Mi Luna – I don't know that we ever reached the potential of this song. I think the chord progression and melody have stuck with me over the years, but my arrangement didn't do it justice.

7. Creep – I was so glad when it was selected because I knew there were lots of people that *needed* to hear us sing it. It was highly controversial when it was debated at Song Selection, but the group finally agreed that the darker messaging/content was something we could use in our dialogue with youth. We were right, and this group of adult women singing those lyrics helped normalize the feelings of isolation and depression. I would've preferred using *all* the original words, but we *are* a

family friendly group. LOL. Emily was the preferred soloist. She kept it simple and put it across so well. Pat's intro also had impact, and I really think the choir was able to reach people with this song...You could feel the impact in the room when we sang it. Even in rehearsal, people would be crying.

8. Is You is or is you Ain't my Baby? - It's not like it's a heavy meaningful song...just plain fun. Fun to sing and fun to play. I actually had a little call bell on top of the piano that I had to hit in time during the chorus! Of course, the group kazoo solo in the bridge was silly too.

9. Lacrymosa – (Yes, the choir has sung in Latin.) I love this piece from the Mozart requiem and wasn't sure if we could pull it off. I was proven wrong, and I loved Soromundi's take on it...One of our most successful efforts in mastering a classical piece.

10. Who Lives, Who Dies, Who Tells Your Story? - This was a huge challenge, both for the choir and for me. *Hamilton* had just been staged and trying to arrange the piece felt beyond me. However, we were able to learn it (over many months) and eventually perform it with the spoken dialogue and costumes. I think there were 5 different soloists?

11. Where is the Love? - I love the fact that we have built enough trust in each other that I can ask these middle-aged women to step far outside their comfort zone into styles they aren't familiar with —like rap. This type of risk taking and courage is what our audiences expect from us each year. It gives different meaning to the songs and their

message when we sing them—there's a focus on the message, on *why* we choose them. For me, this song represents that there's *nothing* heard yet—or that hasn't been written yet.

MY FAVORITE SONG WE NEVER PERFORMED: THE HAMMOND SONG (by the Roches) – I love the song, but it was out of our reach in the early days. However, I would introduce it two times—early in the season when we had a lot of hanging out and joining the choir to pick up girls. This song required all singers to sing super high *AND* low. It's also funny because I didn't even have the lyrics right! I just made them up. (There was no internet and my cassette recorder was terrible. So I couldn't understand the words.)

Honorable Mentions

1. Across the Sea (attributed to Clare Schuman) – our first piece in German...talk about a trust exercise!
2. When Will I be Loved? – The choir loved it... Sound strong and confident. However, it was my first piano solo "off-book," and I was terrified.
3. Museum Cases – Powerful cultural and historical references that moved us *and* taught us about crimes against the First People. We stopped singing this one because they weren't our stories to tell, and we want to respect that.
4. Sing Praise – A simpler melody written by our own Myeba Mindlin. It spoke to me, and I harmonized it for the group.
5. Testimony – Only because I love the reflective mantras by Ferron and every lesbian knew it...so I enjoyed watching the audience sing along. (It was

an easy chord progression, so I could relax and watch them.) This sold me on the choir performing current songs that the audience could relate to.

6. April is my Mistress – I love this Renaissance Madrigal, and the choir learned a lot of things in attempting it. (Yes, I said attempting.)

7. Bohemian Rhapsody – We worked our tails off to do justice to Freddie Mercury; I'll also never forget the video clips of *Wayne's World* that flashed on the screen as we performed it. Makes me smile.

8. This is Not my Home – Powerful content; Even though this doesn't directly represent our stories, we were all impacted by the performance of the prison choir. We wanted to raise awareness and support them, giving them a vehicle to reach an audience. As we stopped singing the words, we lowered the lights and let the video run of each "lifer" telling her story. I'll never forget that.

The "Survey" aka "Who We Are"

For many years, Karm conducted a survey of the chorus and shared those results with the audience during the spring concert. The idea came to her after hearing The Flirtations' song, "One of Us," featured on their first CD. Karm says, "It was an accounting of who they were, their differences, and their similarities. I modeled the survey after that and (most years) called it 'Who We Are.' The choir refers to it as 'The Survey.' My reading was always backed by one of our songs."

In the early years, at a time when lesbians and gays were fighting for their rights, the survey helped connect the audience to the chorus. "Who We Are" became "Who We *All* Are." What follows is the script for Karm's 2010 survey that Karm read to the Soreng Theater audience at the spring concert.

Who We Are! 2010

This is the 8th edition of the Soromundi tradition of the reading of the survey about "who we are." We hope it gives you a glimpse into the differences among us, and the common-alities we share with each other and with you.

You know by now that most of us are Lesbians; 10 are Gold Stars; 6 are heterosexual, 5 are bi, 1 identifies as "queer" and 2 didn't commit.

We are bio moms, adoptive moms, stepmoms, foster moms, and moms to our partners' children. We have over 70 children among us, a whole slew of grandkids, and even one great-grandchild. Only eleven of us have LGBTQ relatives – that we know of.

Now before we get to the fun stuff, there are some statistics I must share. One of us had her OR driver's license issued stating she was "male" and one of us, while using a public "ladies' room," was yelled at for being in the wrong bathroom. 15 of us have been gay-bashed – attacked for being lesbian. 8 have been disowned by our parents, and 13 of us have children who have been harassed for having lesbian parents. I will continue to tabulate these statistics until the numbers are "zero" and I have nothing to report.

There is a 59-year span between the youngest of us at 26 and the eldest at 85 and ethnically, we are all over the map. One of us is the great, great, great niece of Amelia Earhart, one's grandma is 101 and one's grandfather was an Arab tent-maker. One of us is in choir with her daughter and one of us is in choir with her mom!

Eight of us are bi- or multi-lingual, 13 have been arrested, and 6 have been in jail. Interestingly, most of the bi- or multi-lingual people have been arrested. This is why I do this, people: to draw massive, sweeping generalities.

3 of us were high school prom queens, 3 were cheerleaders, 1 was the mascot, 1 was homecoming queen, 2 were on the drill team, and 1 twirls a killer baton.19 were high school or college athletes; none of those were prom queens or cheer-leaders.

One built a tree house in an 80' tall tree when she was 10 years old, one of us built a tiny travel trailer that looks like a Gypsy Vardo Wagon, and 6 have built their own houses; none of them were cheerleaders or prom queens. 5 of us are veterans–more than ever before because we recruit–and 1 of the vets was a prom queen!

35 of us recycle everything possible and 2 of us are Master Recyclers. 9 own hybrid cars. One raises worms.

19 are living with a chronic illness or chronic pain, 7 are cancer survivors, 1 is currently fighting cancer, and 8 are living with a mental illness. 8 of us don't have medical insurance, but it won't be long now! 3 of us had to drop out this year because of physical challenges and are with us in spirit. 2 of us are Oregon Medical Marijuana Program cardholders and at least 20 of us are having hot flashes as we stand before you right now!

At work we are college professors, school principals, editors and compost specialists. We grow your food, drive your busses, massage your aches and pains, teach your children, and take care of you when you are sick. We are accountants, administrative assistants, artists, attorneys, college deans, homemakers, librarians, molecular biologists, realtors, social workers, travel agents, woodworkers, and writers. Several of us are retired.

One was a page in the US Congress. One had to run home from Sunday School in Honolulu on Dec 7, 1941, witnessing tracer bullets in the sky and dodging careening automobiles. One hopped freight trains in the '70s and '80s and survived the longest tunnel in the US in a smoke-filled boxcar. One recently met Joan Jett, who, and I quote, "rubbed her sweat on me!" One has been doing yoga since her senior year in high school...for 42 years! One of us worked at Mother Kali's Bookstore for 24 years. One has read every Agatha Christie novel and one of us wrote a 50,000-word novel in November...that's right! In only 30 days! And then wrote a 100-page script for a musical in April!

One went on a pilgrimage to Haifa, Israel. One fasted and prayed to see the light–and ended up coming out. One built a fifty-foot-long, five-foot high concrete retaining wall, *and* planted 100 seedling trees on her property, *and* built a log cabin from trees she felled herself. Must lay down... In 10th grade, one of us made a three-foot tall heron sculpture out of over 200 paper drinking straws and one of us received Best of Show in last year's Mayor's Art Show.

Every Tuesday night we come together in song, and, to some degree, are rescued by the love of Soromundi: Lesbian Chorus of Eugene. [To chorus] Thank you all for being who you are and [to audience] thank you for allowing us to share...

Who We Are with you in this, our 21st season!

About the Authors

Dr. Kate Barry spent most of her working life as a college faculty member and then administrator. She retired from Lane Community College in Eugene where she taught Women's Studies and directed the Women's Program before becoming an executive dean. She has received awards for her work in education to improve women's lives and was the recipient of the Tennison Haley Outstanding Individual Contribution Award from the Oregon Diversity Institute. She lives in Eugene with her partner Barb and loves singing, reading, gardening, yoga, and travel when not plotting her next great project.

Ann Roberts is the author of twenty-three novels, including sapphic romances, general fiction, YA, and the award-winning Ari Adams mystery series. A three-time Lambda finalist, Ann received two Goldies for Best Mystery from the Golden Crown Literary Society. Ann also received the Alice B Medal for her body of work in 2014. She retired from public education in 2016 to focus on writing, coaching, and editing authors. Eight years ago, she and her wife traded the dry Arizona desert for the rainy Pacific Northwest. When

Ann's not running after their pets, AKA the "fur circus," she enjoys journaling by the ocean, tending to her tulip beds, and watching the University of Oregon Women's Basketball team and the WNBA. Ann loves to hear from readers and can be reached at her website, annroberts.net.

Notes

Chapter 2

1. Raiskin, Judith. "Outliers and Outlaws, The Eugene Lesbian History Project." outliersoutlaws.uoregon. edu. 2023.
2. MacDonald, Heather, dir. *Ballot Measure 9* (New York, NY, Zeitgeist Films, 1995, Netflix)